COLLECTED POEMS

OF ROLFE HUMPHRIES

COLLECTED POEMS ❧

OF ROLFE HUMPHRIES

Indiana University Press   1966

BLOOMINGTON & LONDON

Acknowledgments

POEMS, COLLECTED AND NEW

Some of the earlier poems were first printed in Rolfe Humphries' *Europa, and Other Poems, and Sonnets,* published in 1928 by Crosby Gaige.

"Test Paper" was first published under the title, "Laud for Moderns," with a different final stanza.

Some of these poems were published previously in the following magazines, and acknowledgment is made to the editors of these magazines for permission to reprint them here: *The American Mercury, The American Scholar, Atlantic Monthly, The Colorado Quarterly Review, Harper's Magazine, Harper's Bazaar, The Kenyon Review, The Nation, The New Republic, The New Yorker, Poetry: A Magazine of Verse, The Saturday Review,* and *Voices.* Acknowledgment is due also to Harper & Brothers for permission to use the Latin translations of Edna St. Vincent Millay's sonnets.

GREEN ARMOR ON GREEN GROUND

Acknowledgment is made to the following magazines wherein some of these poems first appeared: *Atlantic Monthly, Botteghe Oscure, The Colorado Quarterly, Harper's Bazaar, The Hudson Review, The Ladies' Home Journal, The New Yorker, New World Writing, The New Republic, Poetry: A Magazine of Verse,* and *The Virginia Quarterly Review.*

LATER POEMS AND TRANSLATIONS

Some of the later poems and translations appear here slightly revised, and, in some cases, with titles changed from the original.

Acknowledgment for permission to reprint is due to the editors of *The Classical Journal, The Colorado Review, The Grecourt Review, The Massachusetts Review, The Nation, The New York Herald Tribune, The New Statesman.*

Also: "Among the Paeligni" and "Rain in Jackson Heights" © 1957 by *Poetry;* "From an Anonymous Latin Poet" © 1956 by The Curtis Publishing Company; "The Unicorn" reprinted by permission of Julian Messner, Division of Pocket Books, Inc. from *Strange to Tell: Stories of the Marvelous and Mysterious* by Marjorie Fischer and Rolfe Humphries, © 1946 by Pocket Books, Inc.; the poems "Tribute for Martha Carrier, Salem, 1962" (1949), "July" (1955), "A Song for Mardi Gras (Variation on a Welsh refrain: Dy garu di a gerais)" (1957), "Under Fortress Crag (A Welsh Legend)" (1958), © in the respective years shown, by The New Yorker Magazine, Inc. _____

Of the poems in this collection, *The New Yorker* first published those appearing on the following pages: 27, 28, 29, 30, 43, 44, 47, 60, 61, 63, 73, 79, 82, 83, 84, 85, 91, 94, 97, 104, 106, 112, 113, 114, 115, 116, 117, 120, 121, 122, 124, 133, 140, 148, 153, 156, 177, 183, 190, 197, 198, 199, 203, 216, 218, 219, 223, 224.

CONTENTS

viii

FROM *Forbid Thy Ravens*

FROM *The Wind of Time*

Later Poems and Translations

COLLECTED POEMS

OF ROLFE HUMPHRIES

EUROPA,
AND OTHER POEMS,
AND SONNETS

EUROPA

The party was no good again!
Only the brilliant girls redeemed
A dull and tedious affair:
What was the matter with the men?
To her, at least, they always seemed
Embarrassed or, perhaps, afraid,
Polite, intelligent, and thin,
Never a bull-necked savage there;
So she came home and went to bed.

Exasperated, she undressed,
Shook back her hair, and tumbled in,
Pulled up the sheet again, and pressed
Its chilly edge against her breast—
She wanted so to be possessed,
And she had really never been.
Her body's manufactured ache
Kept her half-sleeping, half-awake.

She listened to the big old boats,
The ponderous deliberate hulls
Whose hoarse and raucous whistle-notes
Set up a pounding in her pulse:
They were not boats, they were not boats,
They were not boats at all, but bulls
With red and thunder-swollen throats,
They were not boats, they were not boats—

She suddenly switched on the light,
Looked at her body in the light,
Her slender body, slim and white,—
They were not boats at all, but bulls!—
She could not stand it any more,
She flung the bedclothes on the floor,
Swung herself half-around, and rose,
Hurried and firm, put on her clothes,
Slipped down the stairs and out the door.

Out in the street, she heard the blare
More nakedly across the air.
Each bull was bawling to his cow
More softly now, more softly now
Each lowing urgent bull besought her . . .
She turned her footsteps toward the water.

And when she reached the water-front
She saw her monster, huge and blunt;
She saw the shiny river rise
Up to the level of his eyes,
He had his secrets hidden in
The water, and he did not stir,
Firm in his rut he waited her.

She dipped her fingers in the flood,
She dipped her fingers to the wrist,
Oh, what a pounding in her blood!
The water sipped and sucked and hissed
Against the fragile, paper-thin,
Red-hot sheet-metal of her skin,
Preliminary, cool, caressed
The burning nipples of her breast
As, glad because she could not swim,
She started wading out to him.

CALIFORNIA

Spirits, for all they think they can
Survive alone, aloof from man,
Need flesh and blood about their roots.
This land where giant colored fruits
And gorgeous fragrant blooms comprise
A vegetable paradise,
Apparently does not contain
One rich essential nitrogen:
The men who dig this golden loam
Never turn up the smell of home;

Uneasily they sense a dearth
Of dead men, fertile in the earth,
And, while their bodies prosper well
Upon such rank material,
Their thin unhappy souls are whirled
Over a blue alarming world.
Unanchored to the ground, they grow
A little frightened, justly so,
And far too social far too soon
Like men transplanted to the moon
Who skip across the lunar crust
Making friends swiftly, as they must
Who have no relatives at hand
In a bewildering foreign land.

PEDAGOGUE

IN A MILLIONAIRE'S HOUSE

The master of this house has gone
And I am here to watch his son.

Red ivy covers all this home
But inside nothing red can come.

As soon as I come in the door
I feel constrained and insecure:
The soft rugs glide across the floor.

To lofty ceilings blank walls rise
Hung with dull careful tapestries.

No crimson mistresses could sprawl
On these stiff sofas by the wall
Overstuffed, respectable:
But there are comfortable chairs
For rustling portly dowagers.

There are mahoganies and oaks;
There are not very many books.

Though many fires are laid, there is
No room with smoky memories:
On ashless hearths immaculate
Nice logs like foolish virgins wait
Fires that will never come to them.

The lights are neither bright nor dim.

Glass octagons of doorknobs gleam.

Unnoticed people serve my food
Moving the dishes as they should.

I will be glad when he comes home
And I can go back to my room.

DREAM

He thought that he had buried her
   So deeply, deeply underground
That her dead body would not stir
   Nor her stopped mouth make fluttering sound.

And then he flourished like a tree,
   New leaves of grace began to show,
And all his friends rejoiced that he
   Could have, at last, his chance to grow.

But what they could not see nor know
   Was that the silver sap which fed
His brilliant daily strength, would go
   At night down to its old dark bed.

Thus, sensitive in sleep, he found
   That on occasions he would feel

In that unconscious underground
  A palpable, direct appeal.

In an environment that suits
  A readjusted buried soul,
She keeps on tugging at his roots
  Like an unkind, aggressive mole.

RATIONAL MAN

His restless glance abruptly drew
An arc halfway around the rim
Of earth's mysterious big bowl:—
After escaping from his soul
Colors of sleep were standing by,
Their dark-blue shadows all around him.

This was the kind of night, he knew,
That, for no cause at all, would hound him
And set his spirit prowling, prowling—
His glance, grown tired of running, flew
Suddenly upward to the sky
And stopped. The moon gazed back at him.
He stared, frowning a little, scowling . . .

He had discovered that, despite
Supposed advantages of sex,
When that white globe was on the wax
He could not hope to be immune
To lunar influence, nor fight
The monthly fullness of the moon.

And then he saw some poplar trees,
All in a line, set close together,
Essential to a stiff design
In formal-garden symmetries.
He counted them, and there were nine.

9

He thought that they were beautiful.
Then he began to wonder whether
They were, like him, susceptible
To that distinct unearthly pull.
Some influence, he saw, was making
Their leaves keep rustling and shaking
Strangely. There seemed to be no breeze.

Rest and quiver, rest and quiver,
The trembling trees stood close together:
Their false propinquity, however,
Was not surprising to discover,
For he remembered he had heard
Poplars would never touch each other
No matter how their limbs were stirred.

There was a symbol for his shield!

Nine poplars on a moonlit field,
Aloof, fastidious, intense
With shuddering self-preference:
He had no one near him to touch
But the idea consoled him much,
And he, whose lot was not like these,
Took comfort from the popular trees.

DROWNING

Willows that bow
Over dark still water
Are quiet now—
In the windless firs
And the tall pines around
No breath stirs
And there's no sound
Under dark still water.

Down deep
Deeper than sight
Where no lights glimmer
A weary swimmer
Has gone to-night
Has gone to sleep.

Little boats loom
In the hushed night
And slower and slower
Row, pause, lower
A long pole with a light
Down through soft gloom
Down to his room
Under dark still water.

Luminous, dim,
The light has found him
Where black fishes swim,
Poise, and resume
Their slow course around him—
He rests so wearily,
But there's a light in his room
And he rises, eerily

Slowly, in wonder
Groping, asleep,
Suddenly up from under
The dim-lit water
To burst the hush
That had gone down deep
He comes to a boat's side,
Oozy and dripping.—
Arms keep him from slipping.

Was he sleeping there
Under dark still water?
What was he scared about

To make him stare
So wildly open-eyed?
To make his tongue hang out
Like that—?

A LITTLE POEM FOR SPRING

In March I deck my window-sills
With shining yellow daffodils
And almond-blossoms, too, I prize
As sedatives, my soul being wise,
For when Spring starts her yearly riot
And I grow restless and unquiet
Almond and daffodil, I find,
Are very healing to the mind
Because they keep, in spite of hell,
A wholesome truthful bitter smell,
A cynic frankness, which implies
That Spring's mad arts are—simple lies.
Well! Spring can't bring me to my knees
While I've such honest friends as these.

FOR GOOD GREEKS

Midas, desperate for drink
Gulping lava, winced and frowned,
Dumb in torment, being told
Of a cataract of gold
Pouring richly to the ground.

Midas, with his stupid brain,
Only thought of coins that clink,
Hard round yellow disks that bound,
Skip and wheel across the ground.

Pity him, who has not lain
In the rain with Danae,
Known the golden rush that falls
In a room with wooden walls,
Loveliest of miracles!

Golden waterfalls refresh
That dry earth, our arid flesh:
It is beautiful to see
How a human body glows
As the colored shower goes
Deeper, deeper, seeping in
Underneath the thirsty skin.

Orange blood and liquid sun
Mingle in the veins and run,
Run, run, run . . . Rejoice with me,
I have been with Danae!

EAGLE

Head sunk in humpy shoulders, there he sits
Among his little friends, and he is good.
He does not maim nor kill them, as he could,
Clawing their puff-ball fluffiness to bits.
No, he is gentle; all about his feet
They hop and scratch in safety, timid wren,
Garrulous sparrow, plump maternal hen,
And little chickadee, so sweet sweet sweet.

They are ashamed and sorry for him, though,
Because he looks so out of place; they make
Apologetic twitters for his sake,—
"Our poor unhappy brother-bird, you know,
He can not flutter, he can only fly!"

13

At that, he ruffles sulky feathers, blinking
His poison bitter, amber-yellow eye,
And—if he thinks at all—he must be thinking
About the still, thin desert of the sky.

AEOLUS

I am Aeolus, who keep
Or try to keep, my winds asleep.
Good watchman that I am, I know
One at time alone may blow,
Whose wildly jealous kin will rave
Within their black and stifling cave
Unless I turn them into sheep.

And once this miracle is done,
I love my freedom in the sun
Where I may sit, on holiday,
With friends who happen by the way,
And talk and smile, until I hear
Behind my back the sound I fear,
The ominous confusion,—Hark,
My winds are fighting in the dark!

Forgive me if I turn and go
Without one decent word. I know
How rude I seem to every one,
But I must do what must be done,
Unseen and single-handed, fight
Those stormy devils in the night,
Unseen and single-handed, save
The world from ruin in my cave.
Responsible and tyrannous,
Pity me. I am Aeolus.

AGAINST FOG

Rich world of tint and line, of hue and cry,
Of music and motion, counter-plot to Death
Most vain, most valiant, blaze upon the eye,
Come resonant on the ear-drum, and let breath
Be drawn in savor only. Far too thick
This muffled atmosphere, this yellow pall
Wherein we peer and listen, strained and sick,
And calling through the murk as all men call.

Lo, the wild beasts more stately to and fro
Move through a landscape cleaner-cut than this
Opaque dim Paradise of ours, so blurred
By the brain's mist. Where deer and panther go
No grey vapor of nomenclature is,
No film of title coats the colored bird.

SONNET 326

Weary of quests and all such poppycock
Childe Roland to the Dark Tower came once more
With a sigh that called his pilgrimage a bore,
A dull adventure, void of hope or shock.
He yawned wearily, fumbled with the lock
As he had done so many times before,
Then rapped with languid knuckles on the door
Without expecting answer to his knock.

And the world suddenly blazed and flashed and
    shone
With blue-green lightnings; scarlet rivers poured
Rolling floods of bright vermilion wonder:
In the riot, naked and alone,
God Almighty strode across the thunder
Roaring and brandishing a purple sword.

TO THE
GREATEST CITY IN THE WORLD

No permanent possession of the sky
Nor everlasting lease upon the air
Is given any town. *Prepare, prepare*
To see your towers falling. By and by,
Vertical city, delicate and high,
Even your cliffs must crack, topple, and share
The common doom that blunter buildings bear,
Tumble and crumble, disappear and die.

And some day solemn folk, who never knew
Except from ancient hearsay, all your wonder
Of splendid elevating steel and stones
Will come with shovels, rummaging for you,
With dredges pull the river mud from under
Your rusting huddled fragmentary bones.

BELATED VALENTINE

No flaw of softness in the chiseled air,
No flake of grey, no smoky feather shown
Save a warm girl's breath, so softly blown,
So slowly pluming, curl and eddy, where
Hard with a blue intensity, the glare
Of cold-in-mail benumbs the blood and bone:
Under the ice uncolored earth and stone
Fuse in the tight contraction of despair.

What shall be done to keep the crimson heart
Alive unwithered when this lunar chill
Strikes in against its bony trellis?—Go
Stamping in fury, lonely and apart,
Or walk for warmer comfort, if you will,
With a dark girl across the winter snow.

HERESY FOR A CLASS-ROOM

Green willows are for girls to study under
When that green lady, Spring, walks down the street:
Look out the window, Jean, look out and wonder
About their unseen earth-embedded feet.
Under the dark uncolored mouldy clay
Where willow roots are thrust, their life is drawn
Up through the limbs, to burst in bud, and sway
Slow-shaken green festoons above the lawn.

So never doubt that gloom turns into light
As winter into April, or as bloom
Breaks on the barren branches over-night.—
Little enough is learned in any room
With blackboard walls, on afternoons like these,—
O Jean, look out the window at the trees!

HOMO ADDITUS NATURAE

O my young fellow, innocently going
Across earth's colored acres, stride by stride,
Wrapped in your cloak of mood, and gaily showing
A scarf of modern thought, too bright to hide,
Under the trees, and over water flowing
You pass with careless eyes, preoccupied
With what you wear, aloof to stones, unknowing
The pull and power working at your side.

Some day a ragged, curious old man
Will come and sun his reminiscent bones,
Hungry to keep what permanence he can,
The potent trees, the dull magnetic stones,
Still unaware how cunningly they drew
Him into them, long since, when he was you.

17

ONE FLESH

If there were modern magic, she would turn
Into a bullet, cursing, in her pride,
The puny element that let her burn
So hot for impact, so ungratified.
For she knew what she wanted—she would die
Against a rock too strong for her to move,
In battered ripping bitter ecstasy
Kissing the fierce stone body of her love.

But he would be a dull-green lump of sponge,
Soft as wet weeds across her rage, to heal
The threshing fever, check her savage plunge,
Embed in ooze the desperate crying steel—
—Or else an ashy heap of sand, to choke
Her madness with his dusty yellow cloak.

ELIZABETHAN SONNET

Daub ashes on thy Lenten face, and pour
A drink of gall and wormwood in thy glass!
Thy mistress hath deserted thee before,
The more fool thou, to search and cry, *Alas,
My froward darling!* . . . Often hast thou lain
Keeping thy vigil fondly, for her sake,
While Sleep hath crept abed betwixt you twain,
And made of thee a cuckold, wide-awake.

God pity thee, for that thou art less man,
The more thou art a guardian minister!
And for my grudging, jealous self, I can
But envy thee, as thou dost find in her
Some rich reward to keep thee satisfied
For thy poor bruisèd manhood and thy
        kidnap 't pride.

CONFERENCE

Mouth says, "Note well that here the matter ends,
"Life must be snug and standard as before;
"This will not break your heart; we can be friends,
"But lovers never, never any more.
"I must, in self-defence, discover how
"To manage for myself, from this time on."
Mouth says, "Oh, I can do without you now,"
Mouth, spokesman for the Brain, says, "Get you gone!"

And Body, very beautiful and tall,
Mute auditor of speech as grave as this,
Softly comes close, too much concerned to miss
One syllable, making no sound at all,
Wondering if the spoken words are vain—
O Mouth, take Body's part! turn traitor to the Brain!

TO A SATELLITE

I know I am your glory and your sun
And so I am amused when people praise
Your delicately tender little ways
Because I know that every single one,
Confronted by myself, would turn and run
To shadows and to darkness, for their gaze
Would never tolerate my fiery blaze:
But you are restful in comparison.

As for myself—I think—I would resign
All my attraction, if that would make you shine
With your own radiance. I had rather far
You were a homely snappy little star
Than this cool luminous dead thing you are
Oh lovely and beautiful, oh moon of mine!

19

WORDS TO BE FLUNG UP
A STAIRWAY

Never you mind about my milksop heart!
If I no more shall be the full of the door
In your high hallway, O be very sure
That I have learned at least the way to part.
Taller than ever now, and haughtier,
The arrant body smoulders, magnified
And swollen by the hot internal pride,
And saying, "Ha! Well done, well rid of her!"

So to the street, my body and pride and I
Stumble?—not we, but walk the paving-stones
In rage and passion, feeling in our bones,
Under their singing tension, that whereby
We live and nourish our condign estate,
Our final precious food, the marrow-fat of hate.

MAN WITH QUEER EYE-BALLS

The flesh is a cheat, said I, the flesh is a cheat,
A mockery in dumb show, a pantomime
To fool my vision on the sunny street
Or dupe my blindness in a darker time;
Under this acid gaze, this second sight,
Beloved girls who wander to and fro
Turn into racks of skeletons, ash-white,
Who jerk and hitch a little as they go.

And all the old distinctions I have known
And had some faith in, what are they?, I said:
The flesh, a draper's imposition, thrown
Across the ribs; that other hoax, the mind,
A thickish gruel, more or less refined,
Poured in a bony noggin called the head.

LOST YOUTH

I thought I'd like to be back here once more,
But I am sorry. Oh, don't ever come
Revisiting a long-forgotten home
Unless your present manly pride is sure
Not to be vexed when sights and smells remind you
Too vividly of early impotence:
What if a baby ghost should tag behind you,
Rattling a stick along a picket fence?

Poor child, I dodge him. I confess with shame
That I dislike to have him bear my name,
I want no modern friend of mine to know
That he and I were once the very same.
Why should I hate him and despise him so,
That foolish little boy of long ago?

SONNET IN VAIN

Not sick, nor bent on self-destruction either,
I can not sleep for thinking I must die,
The proud warm substance of the body wither,
Turn humble-cold, and I no more be I.
Hot cruelty, sick love, and lonely sleep
Are not so much to live for, nor this murk
So permeate with air and fire to keep
The heart assiduous at its crimson work.

But the doom's wonder of the heavy slow
Swing of the turning world around the sun
Is no mean force that easily lets go,
No paltry fare that hunger gnaws upon.
Son of a rich intolerable swarm
Profusion-bred to die, O Rolfe, stay warm!

OUT OF THE JEWEL

Εἰς βόας ἐν δακτυλίῳ

AFTER THE POET ARCHIAS

Look closely at this little ring
With jasper signet, on my hand:
We do not always understand
The magic of so slight a thing.

In exquisitely chiselled stone
The microscopic cattle breathe,
While on the meadow underneath
Out of the jewel, grass is grown.

EPISODE IN ELYSIUM

In the unending evening, Virgil only
Slowly said, "The wandering begun
Under the dark is always sad and lonely:
Dear boys die young; and pitiful old kings
Stretch in the bloody dust; tall towers are done
To ruin; there are tears for mortal things.
Be fourfold happy now your rest is won."

And all I said was: "There are tears as well
For landscape, and the wonder-working earth
Can touch the mind with sweetness. You were never
Sorry to die, O sorrowful from birth!"

So I, no more. And Virgil, hearing, fell
Silent again, sorry for me forever,
Mournful among the holm-oak trees of Hell.

ET NOS MUTAMUR

My friend's delusion sees
Time move from left to right
By visible degrees
Across the line of sight.

But Time is Space, I know,
Wherein I always go
One way, or, turning, see
A blurred and alien me,

Or hear, behind my back,
Not chariots' attack,
But my own idiom
Grown obsolete, then dumb.

And how shall wit repair
This ravage in the air,
Or will avail to bind
Disintegrating mind?

Ripeness is all.
                    O vain
Richness! Autumnal gain!

MELODY FOR THE VIRGINALS

Contrive to cheat despair
With an old hope
Long laid by;
Cry to alien air—
This is wrong.

This will never help
Nor the salt tear

Be pretty any more:
Now whose song
Tells no lie?

Graces, airs of woe
Suit the unstrung wire
Of a mute harp
Laid by long,
   Who knows where?—
Far from here.

MEDITATION FOR SEXT

Temper to eyes' endurance this unmerciful light,
Coerce the sun with cloud; let shadow range,
Stain, change these areas, this garish plain.

White walls, white towers, white pigeons, unrelieved
By rainbow feather, rain's brown stain, tree's shade,
Blind imperfectible mind with perfect grace.

Fasting, faint, mortal appetite
Craves less than quintessential certitude,
Refrains from alien unfamiliar food:
Give us our daily darkness.
                    Let us pray.

LAUD FOR EVENSONG

Never mind whether air
Stirs, whether leaf
Trembles, whether bird
Makes any song.

Never mind either whether
Coolness freshens the flower
Or fragrance is shed
From the flower shaken.

For here is light
Resident wonder
Whose lovely nature
Has of its essence
Motionless change.

Therefore address
To the hour's presence
Your brief praise.

LYRIC WITH AMBIGUOUS
REFERENCES

*Sorrow and Song and Rust were all entered at
Belmont Park one day in a race for maiden fillies.
They made Song the favorite; but let us say, for the
purpose of the argument, that Rust won the event.*

Sorrow and Song, and Rust
Hath overtaken both:
Sorrow and Song were loth,
But Rust closed strong.

Sorrow and Song go far;
Favor them, fare worse:
Fugitive as they are,
Rust takes the purse.

Men who are all too fain
Follow Sorrow and Song:
Rust comes over again
In the long run.

Sorrow and Song compete
In vain, invite defeat,
As whosoever must
Who doth engage with Rust.

EVENING, A PUBLIC PARK

The lake darkens. The lake darkens. And all those
    men,
The loiterers by stone paths, have all gone home.
They live far from the park. The lake darkens. Again,
O amber and umber sky, O upper air,
The lake contains only your little semblance:
The water holds no other alien substance:
The little boys have taken their sailboats home.
The men have gone. The stone paths are alone.
So—till the lark wakens.

42D STREET LIBRARY

Lunatics love it here; and lovers wait
Standing beside the lions; and poor bums
Come in to read a paper out of the cold.
Suspicion is a portion of this air.
The guards who make inspections at the door
Have subtle ways to persecute the morbid.
Page-mutilators get away with murder.
Around the urinals despairing fairies
Gather like doves to some soiled altar-stone.
Dark motes that circulate in every chamber,
Corpuscular in every marble vault,—
How many are sad! how few indeed exultant
On this grave island in this island's heart.

PISCINA, SINE PISCIBUS

(Roman wing, Metropolitan Museum)

Water, antiphonal to stone,
Falls mute, beset by strait design;
Basin, rectangular as Rome,
Constrains the fluid bent of rhyme;
And marble, murmur's antiphon,
Awaits a shadow never thrown.

ATLANTIC ROUND

The rush and wash of the water along the bows
Reminds me, falling to sleep, of a country house
On a dirt road, on a side hill, inland, far from the
    shore
Where, in the summer dark, heavy and warm, the
    roar
Of wind rising at night makes a surf of the boughs,
And the sound of water is heard ahead of the rain,
And woods with a noise like ocean remind me, again
Going slowly to sleep on the second floor
Of the rush and wash of the water along the bows
Of the ship I am on, deep-loaded, rolling, far from
    the shore.

S.S. Bilderdyk
The North Atlantic, January-February, 1939

VALSE TRISTE

Rich, dark, somber, slow, sad music
Mournful and useless, calls
The sick at heart, the far from home, to harken

3 0

Around the inlaid walls,
(Bright wood, and plush, and palm), attending music
That swells and dwells and falls.

Sunday at sundown, on a steamer cruising
An agèd sea whose weight
Has borne all things but tide, whose acres darken,
(The hour is late),
Whose shores are sunk in even deeper darkness,
Decrepitude and hate.

O to no purpose drowned
Under the seas of sound and sound of seas,
(Sorrowful passengers!), for consolation
Vain, vain as girls who pose upon a frieze
That no one, yet, has found.

S.S. Champollion
The Ionian Sea, April, 1939

GREEN MOUNTAIN SEMINARY

The wide air surrounding
This soft female place,
The open undulant hills,
The naked chance of light,
Meadow and mole and moss,
The pretty little grove
The path, the secret road.

And the tall obelisk
Dial to plain and mountain,
Reminder to the sight
And testament of men
Where only humble males
Tend car and furnace, till
Garden, and water ground.

31

And the young devotees,
Back to the grass, the hand
Flung back across the shoulder,
And the bent knee upraised:
Europa's innocence,
That heat of Pasiphaë's
Dispelled in thoughtful speech,
Gone, to the wide air given.

Yard where no snow-white bull,
With swollen dewlap, goes
Meekly over the green,
Garlanded, bright of horn:
O Majesty! O Love!
But serious ministers
Serve in their several parts,
Safe in their good behaviour.
  Whom virtue gentles, rude
  To mock their decent ways.

Pity. Reject. And praise
The parlor by the track,
The simple fuchsia grown
Beneath the shade half-down;
And praise the railroad yard,
And praise the railroad whores:
Praise ugliness for once,
All that is barren, real,
All that is tough and hard.

THESEUS

—Laberinto, Estela, Arbol, Lucero.

The eyes that faced the Minotaur and the maze,
 Confusion and horror, turn,
For a change, to a simple sight—the wake of the ship
 From a sunny place on the stern,

Looking down and off, all day, at mottle and foam,
In the altering light, as the course is set for home.

After long hours at sea, it is good to hear
        Again the cry of the cock on the low green shore
As the ship moves up to her mooring against the tide,
        Passing the huts of the poor
With a dirty girl on the steps; it is good to see
In the humble yard, the single perfect tree.

And a man alone ashore can lie awake
        All night long, and look at a tree, content
To have that shadow for landmark overhead,
        That substance represent
The simple sense of earth, whose loam and soil
Wave cannot wreck, nor salt contrive to spoil.

And, before too many nights are over, long
        For the multiple mode again, and start to trace,
With the mind's eye roving the labyrinth of leaves,
        The pattern in the maze,
Tortuous in dark night, until there are
No bright stars except the morning star.

Whose single presence, pure in utter space,
Puts in the mind once more the heave and the
        swell
Of infinite sea, and the underground abode
        Where once there used to dwell
Black double horror, overcome and slain
By one with sword, and one with golden skein.

SONG, DIMINISHING

The brave and beautiful
Hear, on their finest days,
The sound of music rising,

33

Or maybe a dream of music,
Sprung from the secret source,
Risen from underground.

The generous and warm,
In clearest weather, see
A lustre laid on the air,
Color beyond all shining,
The brightest kind of storm.

The generous and warm,
The beautiful, the brave,
Perish, are lost, or fail
In the world's perilous war.

The prism, the chord, the man
Resolve their harmonies:
Themselves they cannot save.

Darkness, the ground, the grave
Receive the broken form.

They die, but they have been.

FOR A SHY PARTNER

Sigh no more that silence, given grace
By music, comes to grief as music ends.
Render to music's echo, lost in space,
The compliment that ease of heart extends
To sain the lonesome areas of air.
Unloving your confusion, loving you,
I have no gift of syllables to share,
Nor warrant to bestow them, if I do.

This interval when dancers, pausing, make
Rebellion at their own intent become
A rest in music, use for music's sake;
Spare word of mouth for other idiom.
The parts of speech impair the metaphor.
Sigh no more, sigh no more.

WISE GUY'S SONG

The heart, that obsolete clown,
That pastoral yokel, still
Has a way of having his way.

Silence him, shout him down
Loud as ever you will,
He'll say what he has to say.

Frown at his antic rage:
Chill him with cold rebuke:
Pay him to let you be.

My friend, my simple friend,
Will come to no good end.

SCAPEGRACE

This overt act, a little island
In the great seas of common sense,
Is capable of no defense,
And warm and soft and green, like Ireland,
With politics and solitude
For latitude and longitude.

FRAGMENT, NOT BY PROPERTIUS

Hoc multos annos multae fecere puellae,
  praefuit arte tibi nulla puella sua.
si qua fuit, mea lux, mea deliciosa voluptas,
  dic ubi nunc teneat dura cubile suum,
ut super aeternam possim cubitare supinam
  virtutemque probis ossibus accipiam.

SECOND NIGHT,
OR WHAT YOU WILL

Say, "You are lovely!", say
"Your body's beautiful!"
And nothing left to say
Nor any more to do
But tremble in the dark
Between the flesh and wall.

Lights out, and only light
From the street corner thrown
Across the naked breast;
Hair dark, and lip at rest
Parted from that delight:
The body tried and taken,
The still unproven mind,
O incompletely known!

Who but ourselves will ever
To or from this deliver
Wholly the flesh and mind
To break or stay in season?
Time will not shift in favor,
Nor circumstance be kind.

SONG HEARD IN A NEW HOUSE

Mirror no more the sigh, the care:
No longer be the other I
Beheld through water, in despair,
Seen as in glass, or double air—
Mirror no more the sigh.

But, turning, let reflection grace
Marvels that burn in air, and shine
Material in outer space:
Or give back Sorrow's pure and perfect face,
Mirror no longer mine.

SONG FROM THE GULF

Love from a source admired
Gives a fine pleasure,
Music and measure
Sweetly combining,
Sweet to the sense:
Who, in her senses,
Who, in his mind,
Wants other token
Once having taken
Seizure of this?

Some, who lack choosing,
Drink a dark water,
Brackish and bitter,
Drawn from a shrinking pool,
Salt as the sea:
Love, out of season,
Is a poor food,
But, duly taken,
By the same token,
Sustenance is.

BRIGHT MORNING SONG

O fair morning,
O lovely day!
The branches moving,
The storm all gone,
And my new darling
Across the lawn
In white and green
Coming my way.

So cool, so pure
After night's heat
And swollen rage;
The storm gone by,
This fresher air
Sweet and serene,
O morning fair,
O lovely day!

"O LENTE, LENTE—"

O slowly, slowly!—
But the swift horses close,
All resolution.
The whispering enters into its final hour;
When the door turns in the dark,
And the poor lover goes,
Alone in the little room, O grieving darling,
Forsake forsakenness:
Let the proud heart be sure,
The passion be the power,
The pain become the peace,
Send the great silence after the great music.

APOSTROPHE, FOR THE
SEVEN STRINGS

Te veniente die—

O Thou my morning song, Thee still at evening
I also praise. O gravest loveliness
In the sad hour; O wit and hardihood
Through landscape's green composure; sweet response
To ghost and substance; richness in the rock,
Peace under the cloud, light on the lonely shore;
O morning song, Thee, in the dark, I praise.

TRANSFER OF REALTY

For H.W.S.

*. . . that the grantees shall have full
possession of said land, and that the
same shall be free of encumbrances . . .*

My strength and your grace
At work on this place
Rolled rock and grew flowers
On ground that was ours.

No clause we can read
In the terms of our deed
Projects very long
The gracious and strong.

So tenancy falls
To the garden and walls
Who take what is left
Without thanks, without theft.

Put our signature here
That their title be clear.

NEW JERSEY ECLOGUE

CORYDON

Here in the shade of this abandoned dooryard,
Let's sit and rest. The bus is late, as usual.

DAPHNIS

Time for a smoke. It's comfortable here,
This little breeze. What is there in the paper?

CORYDON

"Heat Wave Continues. No Relief in Sight.
Thousands Jam Parks and Beaches. City Swelters."

DAPHNIS

Nice time we seem to pick for going back.

CORYDON

You said it. Still,—not such a bad vacation.

DAPHNIS

Ten, four, and two I've noticed more than you have.

CORYDON

No bet. I'll match you at it just for fun, though.

MENALCAS

Begin, O city boys, your summer strain!

DAPHNIS

Some small-leaved solitary light-green trees
Convey in summer still a look of spring.

CORYDON

Light, clinging to the under side of leaves,
Hangs like a bronze or silver decoration.

DAPHNIS

The goldfinch, in his bounding flight, keeps chirping.

4 0

CORYDON

The veery's song goes in a little circle.

DAPHNIS

The kingbird shuts his power off and glides
Onto the phone wire for a perfect landing.

CORYDON

The hummingbird shows off before the female
Making a dozen U's before he's winded.

DAPHNIS

A week before they ripen, oats are pale,
Pale green and jade, translucent as a wave.

CORYDON

Oats when they ripen are a tawny color,
More rich and yellow than a stretch of sand.

DAPHNIS

I found a yellow spider on some tansy.

CORYDON

And I, a tiny red one in the bee-balm.

MENALCAS

Continue, city boys, your summer strain!

DAPHNIS

Unseen, the cardinal whistles like a farmer
Calling his dog across an open pasture.

CORYDON

The Morse code of a woodpecker has no dashes.

DAPHNIS

Cut sumach, drying, has an upland smell,
More so than sorrel, timothy, or clover.

CORYDON

You mightn't think water had any odor;
Notice it next time, over the wet stones.

DAPHNIS

While you sit waiting by the corner mailbox,
The cars come past, one every fifteen minutes.

CORYDON

Farm horses look like pre-historic monsters
Seen on the skyline, early in the morning.

DAPHNIS

White cows turn lavender when slanting sunlight
Stains the brown area wherein they graze.

CORYDON

Lavender cows turn white again when evening
Is far enough along, and the sun all gone.

DAPHNIS

The planes drone over daily, east and westward.

CORYDON

The trains run north and south, and the far engine
Whistles at night, familiar, trite, and lonesome.

DAPHNIS

The wind pours through the tree-tops, pauses, pours
Loud with autumnal omens. Hear, oh, hear!

CORYDON

Rain sounds like wind, but when you listen for it,
Only the wind is all you ever hear.

MENALCAS

Home to the city boys, the bus is coming,
Ite domum, pueri,—the company calls you home.

FORMULA

Mention moth and evening sky
Or the glow-worm's spark,
Or the cricket's ticking cry
Pitched against the dark:

Keep it summer-simple; praise
Harbor, house, or hill;
Never overweight a phrase;
Call it what you will.

IN DARK WEATHER

Uncertain wind goes in a circle round
The rank and heavy day;
Cloud is low this morning on the mountain;
The green below the gray
Turns gray itself when all the branches lift
And the leaves' under-side is raised and shown;
The rain, reversed, is a gray mist ascending
Out of the veins of stone.

MIDSUMMER SONG

Brown grain, yellow flower
Ere the August calendar:
Quarrelsome voice, quiet heat,
Dry lawn, dust on lane and leaf:
Noon hangs on from nine till four;
Air demands *Endure, endure!*
Man and wife, at end of day,
Turning to each other, say
How much earlier dark is here.

VERSE, WITH COLORS

Delphinium, bergamot,
Bloom in this summer plot;
Rich red and royal blue
Improve each other's hue.

Lilies, orange and white,
Each other make more bright
With bell and chalice, seen
Above the growth of green.

Blue, orange, white, green, red,
Full summer colors all
Adorn the six-foot bed
This side the rocky wall.

Purple and yellow later
With golden-rod and aster.

UNDER SIRIUS

Fireflies fewer now in the dusk, in the darkness,
Birds more quiet by day, evening dark more soon,
Lull in the garden bloom, and the corn maturing,
                    Month and a half from June.

Month and a half from now, and the air much colder;
Fire indoors at night; no more swims in the pool;
Grapes and the peaches gone; and the noisy children
                    Cheering the team at school.

And the heart that likes to be sad over some of the
        scenes of summer
Finds in town in fall little to mar its grief:
Stone growing cold, the bird going south with the
        season,
                    The turn, in the park, of the leaf.

AUGUST ELEGY

This time is hard as any to endure,
When the full fruit hangs solid under the screen
Of heavy leaves, and landscape, lush and green,
Darkens under the heavy summer cloud;
 Under the loud warm wind, the vine on the wall
Shudders and lifts like rumpled fleece. The fall
Is audible in this wind. *Ripeness is all,*
Ripeness is all. And Plato's ghost again
Singing, "What then?"

Feel the root torn; beyond this mellowness,
Mature and rich, behold the brown of death,
After the leaves lose weight, come loose, come down
Light in the air, no more one shade, but bright
With all the hues of taint, infection burning
Yellow and scarlet stain across the blue
Till the great wheel, faster and faster turning,
Makes all the colors fuse in winter white.

APRIL NOTE,
WITH A SOFT PENCIL

So soft and beautiful the year,
The season centered in the hour,
So frail the little willow leaf,
The yellow maple flower

A man whose heart cannot abide
Coward or liar, looks upon
The day instead, to quit his grief,
To get his hatred gone.

SEASONAL, VERY SIMPLE

So softly by the shaded ways
Tall in the still autumnal haze
    Moving without a sound
    Over the fallow ground

Pomona came, and from the wood
    Whose dark-green laurels were
Older than summer's ruin, stood
    Vertumnus, watching her.

NO ENEMY

Praise to this winter, for its prison-hold
On summer's hostage sun, and captive light!
When branches crack like cannon in the cold,
Hear the austere artillery of night:
Better be met with bitterness, and brave
In charity and chill, than ever go
Where a green season fattens for the grave
Skulkers from ice, and fugitives of snow.

Cherish the blizzard, then, and love the storm
Whose rage is peace, whose fierce white fume is fire;
Take to the heart this cold that keeps men warm,
Harbor this bitter uncorrupted host,
And let the sight, patrolling far, admire
Surf in dark woods, great mountains off the coast.

WINTER SOLSTICE

Look sharp, to see the winter day
    Before the January thaw
Presume upon a longer stay
    Hardly visible, though.

Beyond this light that falls on snow,
  Bright orange on sheer white, behold
The lawn with softer texture glow
  Green under gold.

Watch the bare tree, whose print you know
  Familiar on the single cloud,
Fuse with that rounded shadow, draw
  That rounded shape around
  To cast on summer ground.

FROM THE SIDE OF A HILL

Light or shadow moves across the valley
Whose various hues of green
Alter, under that pressure, fade or darken
Like landscape seen
Lifted or sinking slowly under water.

Beyond this pleasure let the mind not tarry,
No summer movement take
Save wind across the oats, no sound acknowledge
But what the branches make
When the leaves stir and sound in air like water.

LOSER'S SONG

Where wind and light forever alter
The quick invisible scheme of air,
The slower element of water
Presumes upon the use of color
To draw the idle stare.

Through drift of circumstance or season,
Obedient motes, we go
In cloud of mind, or sunnier occasion,
Able to tender Envy her illusion,
Failure her fonder show.

BREAD–AND–BUTTER LETTER,
ON AN OFFICIAL OCCASION

The Minister Plenipotentiary . . . will receive . . . the representatives of the organizations sympathizing with the Government of the Spanish Republic, at the Spanish Embassy on the evening of July 17, 1937, at nine o'clock.

This elegant house the wealthy lady built,
So perfectly appointed. Luxury. Grace.
High ceilings, narrow panels, the dull paint;
Parquet, mosaic, tile, and porte-cochère;
Library, fountain, patio, and garden:
Credit the house with all it meant to be,—
Involute shell, ornate and beautiful.

Here, without equipage or retinue,
By bus and day-coach, four to the taxi-cab,
Deserving people—strange diplomacy!—
Presume to come, in comfortable dress,
Passed by the butler and receiving-line,
To fill the ball-room, hear the chamber-music,
(The trio in white jackets at their playing!)
Listen to eloquence, for once be those
For whom the sumptuous repast was spread.

Or simply go through hall and vestibule,
On the dark lawn, under the heavy trees,
Pleased to move slowly, free from argument,
Pleased to imagine our tall comeliness,

Disturbed to find this hunger in the heart
For ceremonial, for space, for ease,
For conscience to forget to-morrow's meeting.

And comforted to know our kin are here.

O summer warmth! O decent human love!
Here, in the shell of the old, the new world moving.

FOR MY MOTHER

What's this from you—who drink and smoke and
        bet,—
(The favorites to show),—hold down a job
At, is it sixty-five?—and never yet
Gave way an inch to any canting mob?
Let tourists on the sinking steamer sit
Fatuous in the deck-chairs: sure it's rough,
Maybe the life-boats will careen a bit,
But don't you pride yourself on being tough?

If on your Western acre, evil wholly
Seems to engulf the disappearing light,
While the descending darkness gathers slowly,
Forget it: leftward—look!—the land is bright.

"Capitalism still might make it, if—"
Mother, I think you're betting on a stiff.

LINES WRITTEN FOR
THE OCCASION OF A SALE
OF MANUSCRIPTS

Think what went into these—
  Seclusion, craft, and toil:
What fever brought to book
  These pages time will soil!

That, soiled or fading, grow
  Or fade in price with time:
Corrections made by hand,
  Erasures, altered rhyme,—

All these are here for sale,
  Though not for this designed,
The ordering of thought,
  The profit of the mind.

Lucky, to buy and sell
  While men in Spain are dead
Who battle for a world
  Where books may still be read.

Acquire these residues
For more than single use.

League of American Writers
New York, March 1938

A GAY PEOPLE,

fond of dancing and light wines
—old geography lesson

Without a shadow of a shadow of pride
Dead men and women wander on the streets
Of a grey city. They do not lift their eyes

Above the ground they used to call their own
Even to see bright articles in shops
Or peer at paper treatises on love,
Cheap and neglected in the open boxes.

No leaf on any tree. But many statues,
Bone-white and naked, writhing or sedate,
Gaze through the rain at nothing in the gardens,
At nothing at all.

A funny item in the morning paper
Says that in Washington, D.C., a dog,
A pet of the Italian embassy,
Was granted diplomatic recognition,
With all due status and immunities.
Here, Bonnet! Here, Berard! Here Daladier!
Chamberlain, Halifax! (Down, you sons of bitches!)

Trained hounds that hunt with modulated voice
In the late winter sessions.
                              Have your way.
Without a shadow of a shadow of pride.
What's honor? Air. Who hath it? He that died.

February. The Roman month of the dead.

Again the cock crew. Peace with honor, Britannicus.
Pray for us sinners. Not with a bang, but a whimper.
De mortuis nil nisi—

.   *Quando ver venit meum?*

Hearken! O brave, heart-breaking, noble sound!
Do I hear singing somewhere over the mountains?

                    —Arriba, victimas hambrientes!
                    Arriba, todos a luchar!

Paris, February 28, 1939

THE INTELLECTUALS

Aeternum stagno, dixit, vivatis in isto—

There was Cassandra, whom Apollo loved,
To whom, for promised love, he made a gift,—
Always to prophesy truly:
And, for her promise broken, another token—
Never to be believed,

And then there are those men
Who never loved Apollo, nor he them,
Descended from the Lycian ancestors
Who made the water muddy for Latona,
And for their churlishness were turned to frogs
Forever in that marsh.

Brek-ek-ek-ex,
Co-ax, co-ax! Oho, Batrachians,
Isn't it fun to bubble in the puddles?

Always to prophesy falsely;
Always to seem, at least, to be believed.

THE MAN WITH A DOUBLE FRACTURE

Better be grieving over loss and lack
Than grow, from too close presence, mad or mean;
The injured summer soldier struggles back
To face the winter scene
In no less misery for being found
With self-inflicted wound.

Yet to what neighborhood return? The pits
And craters of remorse
Show the familiar quarters blown to bits
And wreck, with downright force,
Forever keeps the line from being true
To-morrow to fresh woods and pastures new.

THE WAR IN THE DARK

*—Sir, in my heart there was a kind of fighting
That would not let me sleep.*

This fighting grows more hideous hour by hour:
Who can be brave against the war in the dark?
Whose wisdom taut enough to generate light?
Harsh conscience, stifled heart, no help at all;
Night without comfort, winter without sleep.
Nervousness rife, love perishing in cold.

Hell is an agony of bitter cold
Whose fang corrodes, whose talons fix the hour
On frozen rigid points, impaling sleep
Forever out of reach, and turning darkness
From time to permanence, infecting all
With chill and idiot doting, void of light.

Illumination or illusion, light
Fails, and is gone, and, residents of cold,
All we can do is hurt each other always,
Improving on our methods every hour,
Struggle, embracing, locked and tight, in dark
Never succeeded, as it was, by sleep.

There used to be a certitude that sleep
Would be a preparation for the light
Of morning, and the day, however dark
The weather, and the year, however cold,
Would yield their season of armistice, their hour
Of decent mercy, compassionate for all.

But now the singers and the dancers all
Are still as stone, and neither wake nor sleep,
Like warriors roused before the zero hour
And shot, and frozen, standing in the light
Reflected from the snow, colder and colder,
Erect in horrible torpor, facing dark.

Love is a witless exile in the dark,
Delirious outcast, wretchedest of all,
Like a gaunt dog in a hallway, out of the cold,
Starving to death through numb and slower sleep,
Hurt only by experience of light,
Foolishly fed in dissolution's hour.

O in this hour, this agony, this dark,
Who knows what light or music, clear to all,
Waits beyond sleep, the other side of cold?

WITH A RESIGNATION, UNTENDERED

Wars and evil abroad in the world, we bicker;
    Energy gone to waste
Hating each other, morose and furious children,
    Caught, shamefaced,

In a deadlock over MacLeish, or the phrase of a
        sentence,—
    Paragraph three, line four;
Follow the party line, or cavil against it,
    Hate or obey the Ninth Floor.

Not even huddled for comfort together, like cattle,
    Or the poor refugees,
Waiting, head down, for the storm to be over, secure
    Under the dangerous trees.

Having done here all I can, I take my leave,
    Elsewhere to find
Strength more enduring than any a league can give
    In my own mind,

On the sunny side of a hill in the afternoon,
    Or in bed at night alone,
Try to develop the terrible strength I need,
    And have not yet known,

Consign my voice to grave and resolute silence,
    Nor add one syllable,
To all this pitiful ugly dissolution,
    And so farewell.

EPILOGUE

To a strange, hollow, and confusèd noise
Heavily vanish—all those presences
That comforted the scene. He stands alone.
The stage is a barn. The stage is like his heart,
Surrendered, deserted, unutterably his own.
There are cries from the wings, and prompting. But
    he stands
Uncomprehending, shouted-at, and mute;
Enduring, not performing. Dumb. The hall
Is also emptied out. People are going.
He knows there should be a soliloquy, and music,
But no sounds come. And no applause at all.

FRAGMENT, RESTORED

from a single line of A. E. Housman

Morning up the eastern stair
    Climbs, and dusk to Asia dives:
Brute and man renew the lives
    Evening shook her drug upon.

Drink the medicine of dawn,
  Start again, be fit to bear
  Yoke and collar, goad and care—
    These are sure, and trouble thrives.

Still the patient brute survives
  Till the wheel of day is drawn
  With the light across the lawn,
    With the light, no telling where.

A.E.H. IN NEW JERSEY

From mead and croft and coppice,
  By stile and stack and fold,
The leaves would blaze in autumn
  When I was young and bold
  Who now am old.

However red and orange
  October colors burn,
The son of man by moonlight
  Will lie awake and yearn,
  And toss, and turn.

And broad awake at midnight
  Will muse upon his ill,
And hear the Lackawanna
  Whistle for Blairstown hill
  And then be still.

Be still, O mournful whistle!
  Bright colors, cease to shine!
Far from the lanes of travel
  Are men with hearts like mine,
  Who see, and hear, and pine.

ELEGIACS

from three sonnets by Edna St. Vincent Millay

I

"Yet in an hour to come, disdainful dust"

At, morose, dies veniet cum murmure nullo
    concubio obscuro mecum erit iste torus.
sanguine torrenti aut potius robigine sicco
    venis exesis serius, a, venies.
serius, a, venies, cui nunc in caespite verna
    suavia vilia sunt, concubitusque nefas:
nocte perobscura, mea lux, sub caespite eadem
    mecum eris et mixtis ossibus ossa teram.
durior hic multo lepido violentior ille
    suavio quam sudor corporeusve calor:
frigida non stuprum vitabunt oscula foedum,
    nox non sola aderit conscia, crede mihi;
vitae nullus adest socius, refugique clientes,
    amisso domino, deseruere domum.

II

"Whereas at morning in a jewelled gown"

Prospera gemmata mane vestita corona
    mordax anxia tunc difficilisque fui,
continuo spissos agitavi morbida casus,
    noctu furor adest; nunc otiosa feror.
bombilat in xystis strepitus clamorque virorum,
    praecipiti in scalis balteus induitur,
quadrupedante gravi sonitu quatit ungula pontem,
    caela serena mihi proferet ille fragor.
non iam lenta quies falso penetralia laedit,
    contempto strepitu intima tuta mihi;
tum demum totam possum requiescere rixam,
    murmurat incolumi somniculosa domus.
donec finis erit, patefactaque ianua mittet
    me dominam Ditis, vel—potiusve—mei.

III

"Moon that against the lintel of the west"

Luna secuta diem diuturnum languida frontem
    seraque cunctaris Vesperis ante fores.
te nimium taedet caeli convexa tueri,
    trita via cupida es dicere, *Terra, vale!*
Caria nonne tuo revocabitur aurea cordi,
    Caria nonne tibi venit amoenus amor?
ast ibi trita gravi cubuisti languida amore,
    ceraque supposuit te remorante diem.
si quid dulce fuit memoranti gaudia noctis,
    per tua teque precor, a, miserere mei,
cui veniente die labuntur lumina amoris,
    cui nunc ante oculos Lucifer ortus adest.
lente, Luna, precor, per nomen deliciarum,
    lente Sol veniat, ne patiare diem!

LIED VOM MEER

AFTER RAINER MARIA RILKE

Old sea-wind, hither blown,
You come to no one here;
But to primeval stone.

Your own age to its own.

Your own rage to its own
Full stop, land-bound, O risen
From purest space, and hurled
Through void and moon-lit world—

Unharbored force, whom none
Detains, however tense
His concentration strives

As the tossed tree survives
A glimmering of your sense
Waving you briefly on.

A SAD SONG, THIS TIME

Now our joy
Dries, or goes
Underground
In the way
Water does:
Who can tell
Where it lay
Sweet and fair?

Who can say
How far under?
Down-a-down
Past the clay,
Past the rock,
Deeper yet,
Deeper still,—
In that fire.

SOMETHING FOR MY BIRTHDAY

Color is lost in snow,
Softness, underground;
I am alone, and go
Walking around
In wilderness and thorn
On the day I was born.

59

Neither water nor fire
Is good in such a time;
Farewell, desire; farewell,
Indolence and rhyme:
The leaf is brown in color
After the brief green summer.

Knowing the season over,
The harvest meager and mean,
Morose and coward lover,
I contemplate the scene
After my simple fashion
With neither grace nor passion.

THE UNLAMENTING

Even the sweet and gentle find
Some tinge of acid in the mind,
Some small residuum of scorn
To use on men who never mourn;

Who never sorrow, never doubt,
Whose pasteboard fibre does without
The normal salt, the simple tear,
Breathing in arid atmosphere;

With fretfulness and petty rage
An unrewarding heritage,
And with no angel to relieve
Their inability to grieve.

IMPERATIVE ADDRESS

To a fine Critical Intelligence

Unweave these over-woven intricacies,
Unsow the salt-sown areas of ground,
Put the pure image where the blank page lies,
Cultivate sight and sound.

Burn the bad essays, keep the decent phrase,
Shelve reference, shore up no spent belief,
Deepen the mine of meaning, covet praise
For being brave, or brief.

SONG

Who fair and softly goes
In good behavior
Along his own right ways

Or tall and comely riding
The white boat o'er the wave
Down the green river

Blown on the wind's favor
Darling of grace, atoning
By certainty of praise
For darker doing.

SONG WITHOUT MUTES

Willow, sway all your silver in the sun;
Swallow, veer warily; wearily, ah lover,
Follow, or heavily sigh for her; run,
      River, forever.

Savor your sorrow slowly, woe shall wane:
Over in Lucifer's luminous valley of yellow
Fever is foolish, all of our lunacies vain,
  Shallow or hollow.

THE PRINCE OF ENTERTAINERS

Ted Lewis, Hippodrome Theatre,
Saturday matinee in the old days

Lucifer, fallen angel, bringer of light,
Have pity on me, an ape in black, who dwell
Performing in unventilated night
Before these cold inhabitants of Hell.
Fury and arrogance are wasted here;
The unresponsive dead, in rows like stone,
Risk no applause, watchful, as if in fear
To start the blood, or rack the padded bone.

Lucifer, fallen angel, fallen star,
If I may not aspire to praise again
Where all the high serene celestials are,
Grave though they be, more bright and fierce than
    men,
Bestow me grace to keep me stern and proud
Here in Hell's infinite half-witted crowd.

SONNET FOR A RADIO AUDIENCE

All you deaf readers of the page, whom sound
Never surprises, put the paper by,
Dial and turn the single sense around,
Indulge awhile the ear without the eye:
Oh listeners in blindness, hear the word

Conveyed in all its purity through space;
Let music play, and metaphor be heard
Without the inquisition of the face.

However good your eyes, they serve you here
Only as men are served who stand before
The oracles in darkness, or draw near
The Sybil's cave, the triply-bolted door,
Or simple seaside wonderers, who fear
The voice below the wave beside the shore.

STATIC

All the foul fiends and demons of the air,
All the dark atmosphere's benighted host,
Banshees in rage, hobgoblins in despair,
Furious ghoul, mad imp, unbrageous ghost,
Asmodeus, Abaddona, Ahriman,
Belial, Cacodemon,—call the roll
Of succubus and vampire, all the clan,
Nis, kobold, dwerger, gnome, djinn, oufe, and troll.

How they all howl and chatter, whine and squall,
Halloo and whistle, yell, snort, gaggle, screak,
Knock, click, and clash, and stammer! How they all
Denounce themselves poor creatures, vain and weak,
Who with intemperate crepitation sue
To keep sweet crooning sounds from me and you.

ANECDOTE IN VERSE,
OR, THE NEW WILL CARLTON

John was a sort of a rounder, not always true to his
    wife;
He chased around a good deal in a loose and promis-
    cuous life;
But Mary was never vindictive, and so she forgave
    him, of course—
It hardly was worth all the trouble to sue for a bill
    of divorce.

And after he died, she was sorry, and a little bit wor-
    ried as well;
She hated to think of him dwelling forever and ever
    in Hell;
So she got in touch with his spirit, through a medium
    skilled in her line,
And she anxiously asked him, "How are you?" He
    said,
        "Don't worry, I'm fine."

"Is it nice where you are?" He answered, "Oh, yes, it's
    wonderful here:
The air is so fresh, and the grass is so green, and the
    water so bright and clear,
The flowers are gay, and the meadowlarks sing, and
    the little white clouds drift by
In the bluest of skies, and the clover is sweet; con-
    tented indeed am I.

"And I almost forgot to tell you that over these
    pastures browse
A hundred or more white heifers and perfectly
    beautiful cows—"
"You seem very happy in Heaven; you sound just
    like Pollyanna!"
"Who said anything about Heaven? I'm a bull on a
    ranch in Montana."

PAPILLIA JAPONICA (NEWM.)

Or, Human, All-too-human

*On observing the ways of the Japanese Beetle
on our grape-vine*

Hardly distinguishes between love and food:
The female, even *in copula,* keeps on eating
And, though my eyes, perhaps, are none too good,
I more than half suspect her of secreting
Some dainty droplet that the male enjoys,
Or does he bite her neck by way of greeting?
And are we, being human girls and boys,
So very different after all, my sweeting?

We are not bronze and green, have no six legs
To get a better purchase with, and you
Have never laid a string of forty eggs,
Nor, for that matter, ever wanted to;
But who, observing us, might not infer
We fed and ate each other, like him and her?

CHIAROSCURO

Here light in sevenfold splendor, far more fierce
Than that poor element we used to own
Before we came here, seems to burn and pierce
In utter force, through artery and bone.
Rage without wrath, what energy is here!
Released, regardless, over body and space,
Pouring full flood through all the atmosphere
Virtue intense, most bright and active grace.

Yet here the people, in more ways than one,
Are dark indeed, and passive; they allow
The shadow of the load to veil the sun,
And bend the back for this, and bind the brow,
Slumber on stone, and on awaking rise,
Somber obsidian in their open eyes.

Mexico, 1938

65

PASEO DE LA REFORMA

Here in this alien autumn, where the season
Becomes more dry than chill,
And leaves are left on many of the trees,
However many fall,

Far from the seven cold stars, now colder nightly,
Here in the high thin air,
A man observes the splendid reign of light,
So bright, so fierce and pure,

And thinks how, back at home again next summer,
Given expected luck,
Writing to friends, waiting for mail to come,
Killing time with a book,

Not any more a tourist and a stranger,
Where maple shades the stone,
The mind will dwell on floods of light, like rain,
That fall in Mexico.

Mexico City,
Autumn, 1938

INTERVAL

For Theodore Roethke

Between the swung rope and the sound of the bell;
Between the sight of the bird's expanded throat
And the beginning of the treble tune;
Between the flight of the spray and the full roar
As the big comber breaks along the shore:—
Comes the long infinitesimal pause that makes
More music, maybe, than the single note,
Too fine for any but the finest ear
Ever to catch, and hear.

BLACK, ORANGE, WHITE

At Ocotlan I saw the torches flare
From the train window, orange on black, at night,
Orange over orange, fire on fruit,
The trays of great bright globes going window-high
Along the wall of cars, and the ground all white,
Sand in Mexican moonlight, cold enough for snow.

This comes home, as I stop my car in line
On the dark state road, in an hour when snow begins
To dust the hard concrete, and the mountain slopes
Are white except for the ledges and the trees;
And torches flare over black river water
Where troopers fish for a suicide by drowning
And bring him, cold, to the cold Connecticut shore.

"ALL ON A SUMMER'S DAY"

For Marjorie Fischer

Moving like music over the dull water,
Double device upon the shield enlarged,
With a golden wake that goes where he has gone,
Or poised below the willow along the margin,
Before the gaze of the bronze maternal angel,
Looking down at the lake of silver, lingers
Lovely and proud and innocent, the swan.

And overhead that other exercise
Of loveliness and innocence and pride,
The gay and mortal music, played by men,
Made by the human breath and human fingers,
Rises and floats or pauses in the air
Above the listening people, still as the water,
With the merest ripple of motion here and there.

The undercurrent holding up the tune
Clear and simple as light and air and water,
In Central Park on a summer afternoon.

PROTEUS, OR, THE SHAPES OF CONSCIENCE

This is Proteus, a god. He comes from the ocean
Sometimes, at hot noon, and crosses the beach
Looking for inland shade. If he comes within reach,
As he may, dive at his knees; do not be afraid
To bring him down to the sand with a flying tackle
And bind him, overthrown, with the rude compulsion
Of manacle, shackle, chain. And even so,
Ride him hard with your weight. Do not let go.

This god is worse than sly. In your hands he will turn
To utter fire, and roar in your face and eyes;
Or burn, burn like a beast, lion or tiger, bright
And hot and rank; or a lewd and ugly boar;
Or some unshapely horror, moist and brown,
Repulsive pulp to touch, and foul to smell;
Or he may be a lovely river of silver
And blue and green, with delicate wave and ripple
Over the mottled pebbles.

                    Hold him down.
Until the miracle do not let him go.

The final change you will never understand.
You will not know how he ever managed to rise,
Nor how you rose yourself, to find him there,
An upright natural presence, facing you,
As tall as you, in the soft ambrosial air,
Smiling, and looking you straight in the eyes, like a
    man,
And telling you what it was you wanted to know.

6 8

A MAN ON THE ISLE OF PALMS

Looks at his watch, or turns to watch the sea,
Or see his little son
In a blue sweater, tossing a blue ball,
Bright in the southern sun,

Unconscious of the dubious presences
That haunt his father, come unseen, and go
Along a strand that Dali might have drawn,
A beach described by Poe;

Grey sisters, fatal modern goddesses,
Neurosis and Nostalgia, at his side,
Lean fondly over his shoulder, make him love
The slack and ebbing tide:

Whom he can learn, with patience, to dismiss,
Hush the long argument between the cells
And nervous mind; and rise, and walk the beach
Looking for lovely shells,

Or sit, content, and smoke, and feel the sun,
Watch the blue ocean, or shade the page and read,
And study Time and Silence, that great pair
Of which all art has need.

"RÜHMEN, DAS IST'S"

For one who harbors confusion

The apartment not too warm this July morning
For all its summer look—the rugs removed,
White slip-covers over chairs and sofa.

Morning's offer of truce still fresh enough to believe.

You at your desk, preparing to write till noon,
Prolong the indulgent sweet last-minute idling,
Turn in your chair, observe the mountain-laurel,
Note the one flower fallen on the floor,
Admire it for its fresh serene exactness,—
The purity, the purpose, the precision!

And praise the flower, and the god Apollo.

THE SUMMER LANDSCAPE

THE IMAGE

Some trick of light, in the apartment past the court,
Shows me a figure standing by the window,
Hooded and robed in black, and very quiet,
Hands folded at the waist, and golden light
Falling on hands and face.

Not altogether accident. I know
My own imagination and desire
Have made me see this angel, motionless
Yet moving; grave; but breathing, not a statue;
Observer without menace.

And his name
I think I know—his name is like my need:
Composure, who receives illumination.

FOR AN ALMANAC

Dissonance, winter, hate
Combine, conspire, contrive
Against the senses five:
Whining and wailing
Fall on the ear;
Ravenous vanities root in rotting snows;
And the gray day, failing,
Leads to the long white night, and no repose.

Patience, patience, patience.

Oh, and remember
The other side of the year,
The opposite of December,
With laurel wild, and cultivated rose,
With shade outdoors no January knew,
With shade outdoors no February threw,

With the rooms inside more dim,
By noon and afternoon,
Because both trees and awnings interpose
Their comfort, rich or trim,
Or thunder-clouds come over from above.

But the light is bright when we wake up in the
    morning,
Making a little tune,
Taking, for each bad word, its antonym—
Summer, music, love.

Patience, patience, patience.

THE EXILES

Lie in the darkened room and hear
The voices in the street at night
Beyond the open window, talk
In a foreign language, and a strange
Foreign cadence in the walk.

Or look at half a dozen coins
Counting them carefully and slow
To pay for magazines or meals;
This does not seem like money, though,
Nor feel the way real money feels.

Nor is it any longer true
They change the sky, but not the mind,
Who run across the sea, and live
Expatriated, fugitive,
Leaving their land behind.

For the mind changes more than sky,
Becomes infected, covets grief,

74

Craves, but rejects, the newer loam,
Still clinging to the old belief
Of some day going home.

The resolute, who used to form
Firm ranks against the old regime,
Move in a nightmare kind of dream
Where every comrade is a spy,
Each new report another lie.

And those most sensitive and tall,
By that same virtue, dwindle more;
Having a longer way to fall,
Become much worse than men who were
Below their worth before.

The nerves are bad, and tempers flare
In petty quarrels, mean intrigue:
Jealousy and suspicion leer,
Organization is undone,
One against all, all against one.

Talent becomes a show-off ape,
Honesty sickens, having had
No offer to betray the cause:
Why not? Corruption feeds the poor—
If poor enough, all men turn bad.

Demoralized by shattering fears,
Braced against pressure night and day,
The last collapse surprises most;
Disintegration makes the ghost
Even from himself an émigré.

This is what happens, not alone
To men from Germany and Spain
And other lands remoter far,—
We have this sickness, wish in vain
We were not exiles. But we are.

BLACK LYRIC

Love that gives or takes
Regardless of the mind
Cherishes the darkness:
Though the sleeper wakes,
Still the eyes are blind,
Blind, and also needless.

Beauty in the act,
Terror in the cry,
Summons dark beyond
This in which we lie.

Where the red and black
Fuse in utter night
And the other four
Join the sense of sight,
If the awful door
Close or open, heedless.

LA BELLE DAME SANS MERCI

Three of us walking, and two of us were tall,
  Walking, in this dream,
On a down-hill path, in a grove of laurel and pine,
  On our way to a pleasant stream.

  —Who is the third who always walks beside you?

And the third was not so tall, but her eyes were clear,
  And her look so sweet and mild
That rather than wife and mother, she seemed to be
  An innocent-hearted child.

  —Who is the third who always walks beside you?

We paused on the path, though the green and lovely
    wood,
  For a moment, in the dream;
We had plenty of time, we felt no wise compelled
  To rush to reach the stream.

And all of a sudden she raised her ringless hand
  And pointed straight at me,
And cried, "How ugly and horrible he is!
  Look for yourself, and see!"

"Look for yourself, and see!" she cried aloud,
  In rage and fright, and you,
Obedient to her voice and gesture, turned,
  Looked, and saw it was true.

I was no more I, but a lewd and evil shape,
  Coarse-grained and dead as stone,
And the sight of the utter stark and staring truth
  Numbed you in every bone.

And she held the pose, and she looked at you, and
    smiled,
  Turned over her hand, and screamed,
Screamed, and vanished: and you awoke, alone,
  To face what you had dreamed.

  —*Who is the third who always walks beside you?*

TWO LYRICS OF ENDURANCE

I

And now
The white snow lies along the bough
Where once the lovely light was laid
And the long leaf hung down,
And the shade it made is gone.

In this bitter season
Of wan illumination,
Mean temperature, and snow,
Wait; and remember Deor—
This, too, will go.

II

Not like a rock in the stream
Worn away, worn away
By the inveterate water
Day after day after day

But like a tree that stands
By the side of the water, so,
So we shall not be moved,
We shall not be moved, but grow

Taking the life of the water,
How slowly, how late,
Sentient above the confusion,
The spume and the spate.

COMING HOME

You are coming home at night:
You pass from light to light,
Walking around the block,
And your shadow swings to the right
The way the second hand
Goes round a modern clock,
And other shadows, bound
To your footsteps, climb the walls,
Or jerk along the pavement,
And some contract and darken,
Others lengthen and fade.

The lights are various loves
By whom you find your way,
By whom you see and move:
They lend you guidance, they
Enable you to find
Not only house and door,
And wall and window-blind,
But something less and more,
Your image, multiplied,
Cast for your gaze, and thrown
Distorted, but your own.

And what you need the most,
O walker in the night,
Is to continue, sure
The self is really there,
The self is always right,
And neither caricature,
Nor unavailing ghost.

And if a light is broken,
If one of them goes out,
As well they may, of course,
And substance takes from shadow
Its absolute divorce,
Be reassured, in darkness,
The self is never lost.

SPRING PIECE

The golden haze around the willow
Thickens, and all that blue and white
That once were in the snow, have passed,
Have been absorbed by cloud and light.

As snow by warmth is overtaken
The season's slow correction comes

With green for brown, and bloom exploding
In sulphur color through the elms,

In deep maroon among the maples,
And these, in turn corrected, soon
Become the heavier, darker verdure,
The shade and foliage of June,

July, and August, and September,
And that is far enough, I feel,
To let the mind's anticipation
Ride on the seasons' turning wheel.

FROM MY TRAVELS

At Avignon I saw a swan
Whose head was black and white: the eye
Was centered where the colors met;
The eyelid, closing from below,
Was white, the eye as black as jet.

Near Ventimiglia, by the shore,
Not far below the railroad track
I heard the shingle margin make
A grinding sound, and stir, and shift
In water, as the wave went back.

Eastward I sailed across those seas,
And in the streets of Corfu saw
More idiots than I thought could spawn,
The commerce of the centuries
Of sailors, drunk, in bed with whores.

I climbed a hill, and further on
In a museum, on a frieze,
Apollo, perfectly serene,

With blank and eyeless vision shone,
Expressionless above the scene.

Above the rapes and ravagings,
Above the violence and blood,
Above the river-gods that lean
With slimy bellies in the mud,
The great Apollo, gazing, stood.

I heard the wind go through the pines
Where the Olympian runners raced,
And such a hound as might have sired
Ithacan Argos, crossed a ditch,
Snuffed at my heels, and then retired.

The little Æsculapian snakes
Fled from the stones to marshy ground
On Delos, and anemones
Were scarlet gouts among the grass,
Reminders of Adonis' wound.

Along Piræus' darkened wharves
The Easter Eve procession wound
By the black ships; the music played
Slowly, and it was bronze in sound;
The torches made the water bronze.

The bees in Agamemnon's tomb
Were wingèd Furies, multiplied,
Diminutive, but harrying still
Not only his majestic ghost,
But tourists who profane that sill.

I noticed Judas-tree in bloom,
And in a field near Sparta, saw
A goat with wicked yellow eye,
A trousered hawk upon a post,
Indifferent as the bus went by.

Windmills on Myconos; and broom
Like golden fleece on Sunium's height;
The lovely curve of Nauplia bay;
Stromboli's bonfire in the night,
As I sailed westward toward Marseille—

These are the scenes my notebook holds
And I recapture once again,
Turning from page to window-pane,
Watching New Jersey marigolds
And listening to New Jersey rain.

GARDEN PIECE

Day lilies look like flames held up by water:
They flutter, toss, and burn
Irregular orange over the tall green stems
That rise without return;

Like jets from the fountain's many perforations
The tall green rods arise,
And the bladed leaves are water curving over
After the impulse dies.

But the colors are not quite right for fire and water,
Rather, like those that bloom
On the papered wall of a country-town hotel,
Or in its dining-room

In a picture painted by some wretched artist
Who left it, when the oil was barely dry,
To pay for a roast-beef sandwich, a cup of coffee,
And a slab of home-made pie.

THE SUMMER LANDSCAPE

On the stone terrace, underneath the shade
Of the perfect maple, I watch the summer scene:
Beyond the strip of lawn the strip of garden,
Tall flowers, yellow and blue and red and orange,
Day lilies, bergamot, and coreopsis,
Delphinium, phlox, and marigold, and foxglove,
And low alyssum, white against the green.

The side hill falls away, and a point of woods
Comes in from the right, and a little farther down
Another from the left; then rolling hills,
The colored counties; corn, and oats, and wheat,
Dark green, light green, light brown,
One or two red barns, no sign of a town,
Far to the north, the long blue line of mountain.

I am alone, do nothing but sow my fancies;
I am alone, and the afternoon is long.

And the light darkens, and the color changes,
Turns livid green, or cyanotic blue,
And I am less alone now, for a throng
Of people is coming out, a twilight crew,
Who spring, like the men of Cadmus, from the ground.
I sowed them earlier in the afternoon.

The ugly and mean, who sit in grim dejection
And speak no word, nor utter any sound;
Self-pitiers flinging themselves face-down in tears;
Matricides and murderers in the bushes;
Cowards whose bowels loosen at every noise;
Voyeurs who watch for animals to couple,
And when the act occurs, their heart-beats pound;

School-girl seducers, lovers of little boys,
Impotent suicides hanging themselves on trees,

Adulterers hunting women whose open kiss
Has a taste like that of water in a jar
Where flowers have stood too long,—all of them are
Thick around house and orchard, brothers, fighting,
Slaying, and slain; and I am all of these.

POLO GROUNDS

Time is of the essence. This is a highly skilled
And beautiful mystery. Three or four seconds only
From the time that Riggs connects till he reaches first,
And in those seconds Jurges goes to his right,
Comes up with the ball, tosses to Witek at second
For the force on Reese, Witek to Mize at first,
In time for the out—a double play.

(Red Barber crescendo. Crowd noises, obbligato;
Scattered staccatos from the peanut boys,
Loud in the lull, as the teams are changing sides) . . .

Hubbell takes the sign, nods, pumps, delivers—
A foul into the stands. Dunn takes a new ball out,
Hands it to Danning, who throws it down to Werber;
Werber takes off his glove, rubs the ball briefly,
Tosses it over to Hub, who goes to the rosin bag,
Takes the sign from Danning, pumps, delivers—
Low, outside, ball three. Danning goes to the mound,
Says something to Hub, Dunn brushes off the plate,
Adams starts throwing in the Giant bullpen,
Hub takes the sign from Danning, pumps, delivers,
Camilli gets hold of it, a *long* fly to the outfield,
Ott goes back, back, back, against the wall,
        gets under it,
Pounds his glove, and takes it for the out.
That's all for the Dodgers. . . .

Time is of the essence. The rhythms break,
More varied and subtle than any kind of dance;
Movement speeds up or lags. The ball goes out
In sharp and angular drives, or long, slow arcs,
Comes in again controlled and under aim;
The players wheel or spurt, race, stoop, slide, halt,
Shift imperceptibly to new positions,
Watching the signs, according to the batter,
The score, the inning. Time is of the essence.

Time is of the essence. Remember Terry?
Remember Stonewall Jackson, Lindstrom, Frisch,
When they were good? Remember Long George
    Kelly?
Remember John McGraw and Benny Kauff?
Remember Bridwell, Tenney, Merkle, Youngs,
Chief Myers, Big Jeff Tesreau, Shufflin' Phil?
Remember Matthewson, and Ames, and Donlin,
Buck Ewing, Rusie, Smiling Mickey Welch?
Remember a left-handed catcher named Jack
    Humphries,
Who sometimes played the outfield, in '83?

Time is of the essence. The shadow moves
From the plate to the box, from the box to second
    base,
From second to the outfield, to the bleachers.

Time is of the essence. The crowd and players
Are the same age always, but the man in the crowd
Is older every season. Come on, play ball!

NIGHT PIECE, IN THE COUNTRY

The great tree moves in its sleep,
And moonlight pours around
The white boards of the house

And the grey-looking ground:
The great tree moves in its sleep,
And lunar shadows, slowly,
Wheel, extend, and creep,
While silence, pure and deep,
Breathes *Holy, Holy, Holy,*
And *Hush, oh, Hush,*
So the sleeper may not hear
The usual rain and rush,
The motes of casual sound
In the unconscious ear,
But deeper under than ever
In the cool blue room
Slumber, or if he seems
To stir, he is turning over
Only, so, to resume
Knowing the healing dreams.

THE GOOD SWIMMER

The strongest swimmer, the first one over, comes
Wading the last few yards, and over the sands
To firmer, greener ground. And there he stands
Clean from the water, clean in the light and air,
In his own element, with another light,
Not out of time, but his own glory and pride
Shining around him. He raises both his hands
And runs them over his hair,
And down his sides, and lifts one hand again
To shield his eyes against the river's glare.

And watches the struggle, and tries to count the rest,
Heads bobbing, no two together, some halfway over,
Some more, some less, upstream and down, the gleam
Of the wet arm or breast
Fighting the current, or letting it sweep them close

To the jagged rock that lies below the stream
With deep and quiet water all around,
And some tread water till a log goes past,
Or, tired, turn over and float a little while,
Themselves like driftwood, thrash again, and swim.

And he grows tired of watching. He sits down,
Gets up again, and takes a few steps nearer,
Impatient and a little scornful, calling
"Hurry up, come on, snap out of it, you guys!"
Frowning at the river,
He sees the river, running swift and brown,
Under the livid cloud, and darkness falling,
Nor will it come as any great surprise,
At least, not any great surprise to him,
That some of the weaker ones should sink and drown.

THE CONTENDING TWINS

The Ephesian and the Syracusan take
Their exits and their entrances in me
Who serve them both as character and scene,
But the plot is not like that of Shakespeare's show,
No laughing matter of a golden chain
Or a husband kept from dinner. And I know
Their natures differ: one is evil and mean,
A murderer, a man who wants to die,
Or better still, being desperate, be slain,
Yet—oh strange paradox!—will fight to save
His sickly life, will kill me if he can
Rather than let me put him out of his pain,
His wretchedness and misery; the other
Is gay and wise and altogether sane,
My friend, who wants to save me from his brother.

The saver is patient, but the stalker cunning,
Knows how to hide or place himself, to be

Mistaken for the good one, adopts his pose,
His tone, his dress. And, anyway, who knows
Which one is which, they look so much alike?
I am never sure, and this confuses me,
I am never sure, I never really know,
I dare not lift my hand, I dare not strike,
Suppose I laid my benefactor low?
I dare not strike, I dare not lift my hand,
Like some one else in Shakespeare, here I stand
Irresolute, as if Hamlet found his way
Further to block the action of our play,
Already too obscure and dubious
With Life, not Sleep, as Death's Antipholus.

VARIATIONS ON A THEME
BY E. E. CUMMINGS

"What becomes of those who are not artists?"
"Nothing becomes of them. They don't become."
Blind to the motion of the dancing atoms,
Deaf to the music of the spheres. And dumb.

What becomes of lugubrious neurotics?
Nothing. They seep and stew in their own juice.
They go to bed with their fathers or their mothers,
Or plug away at continual self-abuse.

What becomes of the frivolous and frightened?
Nothing. They skate full-speed and get nowhere
Over thin ice, or are blown to tattered fragments
Like the dry leaves in the rushing autumn air.

What becomes of the hateful and aggressive?
Nothing. The males, with bulging eyeballs, crouch,

And the females look and sound like whorehouse
     madams
With a raucous voice and a never-ending grouch.

What becomes of hysterics and compulsives?
Nothing. They scream in their cages, day and night,
Expressing themselves like parrots or hyenas,
Rattle the bars, and want to get out and bite.

What becomes of the ones who look in mirrors?
Nothing. They spend a lifetime, standing there,
Bemused and lost, and colder than stone, being
     frozen
And mortified by their own Medusa-stare.

What becomes of the hypocrites and cowards
Afraid to face the enemy within?
Nothing. They go to the wars, and come home pious
Community bores, who perish in their sin.

What becomes of all of the jerks and phonies?
Nothing, nothing, nothing, nothing at all.
Fame's incorruptible silence passes over
Their bandaged eyes, and their backs against the wall.

L'Envoi

So, forgiving ourselves a little smugness, darling,
And more than one occasional minor lapse,
What we can do is mind our proper business,
And some day get some good work done. Perhaps.

THE VOICES

A voice out of the summer landscape said
"Take it as it is; and do not borrow
Anxiety or sorrow.
Order imagination; have it make
Not rotten fantasy, but happy art."

And another voice out of the summer weather
Said, "You are better than all of them together;
Why tear yourself in pieces for their sake?"

And still another said: "You are strong; be stronger."

And a fourth suggested: "If you have to bother
Keeping yourself stirred up, if you really hunger
After emotion so much, why, vary the diet,
And what's the matter with anger?"

And the fifth voice said only, "Quiet, quiet!"

And all the treacherous destructive devils
That yelled or muttered in vindictive riot
Or quarreled, evil-tempered, in my heart
Could not drown out the seven invisible Sibyls

Whose voices blended under the summer cloud,
Who spoke one phrase together, aloft, aloud,
"For Christ's sake, Rolfe!" across the summer field,
And I was healed, or, anyway, almost healed.

MEDITATION

To take experience, oh, absolutely,
To suffer and succumb,
To let the waves and the billows go clean over,
Still feeling, never emptied-out and numb,

And then to know the arrival of the moment
When one, still taking, must no longer take,
No longer have experience, but give it,
As artist and creator, make

All that one knows, and all that ever happened,
Serve the one purpose, unified in art—
This, to be sure, takes more than doing homework,
Takes brains, and nerve, and heart.

But if the Holy Ghost has finally taught us
To know this much, so far, so good; we must
Expect the working of the power and glory
With confidence and trust,

Humbly, not vain of the gift, nor proud of the
        presence,
But glad of these, and serious, but not grim,
Have fun, and love, and laugh at jokes, and really,
Always, rejoice in Him.

RAIN IN FORTY-EIGHT HOURS

This kind of day streams over us like water,
With water's clarity, light and sound and smell;
The leaves take on a gloss like dark-green china,
Scalded and polished well.

Not only around and over us the bright river
Washes, but through our very flesh and bones:
Why not? Is our material so solid?
Are we men, or grey impervious ancient stones?

We feel this weather, right as Mozart's music,
Moving and luminous, profound and gay,
And come to life, or welcome its invasion
This kind of day.

MAYBE

Do you suppose that a hundred years from now
    Descendants and/or strangers, living here,
Will have the gift of vision, to see us moving
    The way we did this year

About the house or garden in the morning,
    Me in blue, or you in brown,
Weeding or spraying, or typing at the desk
    Upstairs, or lying down,

Reading a book, and both of us impatient
    With the other's ways, inadequate at best,
You irritable, tired, and hyper-active,
    I lazy and depressed,

Unfaithful so, and obdurately single,
    Yet not quite undevoted, being bound
To this economy, and that profession,
    This boy, this house, this ground?

Or late in the afternoon, on the terrace talking,
    With a cigarette, and some pretty awful gin:
What kind of meat should we get to last till Thursday,
    And when does school begin?

Will they see us so? Will they ever really figure
    Who washed the dishes, and who built the shelves,
Distinguish what was man from what was woman,
    Or will the separate selves

Blur into one identity and leave
    A pattern barely able to be traced
In the set of a garden bed or some lines of writing?
    Will they despise our taste,

Or find it strangely like their own?—surprising!
    Scorn the improvements that we thought we made?
Will they reconstruct from the rotting stump the
        maple
    And the slow-wheeling shade?

Will they be skeptics, or believe in spirits
    In 2043,
Kind to the ghosts so surely, surely haunting
    The site of that old tree?

Probably not, judged by our own example,
    Who are hardly ever curious, or care
About tenants past, and in any time or household
    That gift of vision is rare.

And John, grown up, may not have any children,
    Or his sons and daughters die
In another war, with much improved destruction
    Familiar in the sky

And the place which had no heir and found no
      buyer
    Be taken over by wilderness and rust,
While the Latin texts and books about the Russians
    Gather coeval dust.

The sumach, the bramble, the Queen Anne's lace
      will flourish
    With thistle and other weeds,
Untouched by sickle or scythe, in the old enclosure
    Where once were planted seeds.

The wasps will build in the sagging eave and rafter,
    Paint flake, and floor boards rot,
And children, never too late for faith in hunting,
    Will find an iron pot

That will still hold water or sand, or, even better,
    Some clock-wheels, or some springs,
Or a rusty jack in the old garage foundation
    Where the poison ivy clings,

While their folks, who came in helicopters maybe,
    Take berries or grapes, long after we are gone,
Leave paper plates, or lose the thermos bottle
    In the hayfield that was lawn.

Oh, well; no matter what we think about it,
    It will all no doubt come out some other way,
And I put this down, by no means melancholy,
    But reconciled and gay.

FROM THE NORTH TERRACE

(Mid-afternoon, second Saturday in October)

Like a football team whose colors are gold and scarlet
This wedge of trees in fall
Troops out to the edge of the field, with one big
      fellow
Looming above them all

Like a giant tackle whose name is Pug or Butch
And the smaller dark-green firs
Stand around the pack and get in the way
Like school-boy worshippers.

The resemblance will not hold another fortnight
When the leaves have left the bough;
It may not even look, tomorrow morning,
The way it seems to now.

Dismissed from the mind in winter, spring, and
      summer,
As sure as the year again
Reaches this point, it will bring this image with it,
Twenty more times, or ten,

Or maybe less, but if I am there to see it,
Each year, a bit more tall,
These trees will troop to the field, in gold and scarlet,
Like a football team in fall.

THEY TALK ABOUT THE WEATHER

"Leaf going, and light going, and cold coming,
How can we ever bear
November again, November,
Wan sky, chill air,

9 4

And darkness coming down
Earlier every evening,
Darkness over the town
At five, or half past four,
And darkness late in the morning?"

"Not less light then, but more,
Because the intervening
Awning and plush of shade
No longer comes between
The sun and the shining ground:
And have you never found,
Late in the year, a corner,
Facing south-east, and green,
A summer strip mislaid?

"The worst for me is the time
Of the winter holidays,
The sodden slush of the mind,
Then bitter, bitter cold,
The ice and the sleet and the wind
With pocked and hardening snows
Under the grapefruit rind,
And the meager steam of the breath
Against the rigid air."

"Ah, but the light is there!
Notice the way it grows:
What if the temperature
Drop to the zero mark?
Measure increasing cold
Against the lessening dark,
And hear the season's music
In counterpoint combining
Endurance, reassurance.

"A restless rest: then,—fine,
Single and clear and pure—
The melody starts again,

And light and warmth are one,
And light and warmth are sure,
As spring to summer swells,
To the roundness of the year,
Till the lingering music dwells:
Is it changing? can you hear?"

"The counterpoint resuming!
Only this time the stress
Of hot July and August
And the slack of light, grown less,
Grown less, on shore and orchard,
Grown less, and the music softer,
Leaf going, and light—we know,
Having heard, not yet too often,
How these four movements go."

SEASON'S GREETINGS

Not the obvious choice
In days that are over-ill
The over-cheerful voice,
The sentimental phrase,
Not the false good-will
But something in the will
Like steel, as hard and cold,
Resolute and cold,
Pitiless and cold,
Passionate and cold
As bitter zero weather
In winter's shortest days.

Some are off to the south,
Others to the wars,
Others fight the wars
Only with the mouth.
These are not our wars,

But on our proper ground
We will not malinger,
We will not retreat,
We will not desert,
We will not be cowards,
We shall not be found
Threatening or howling;
We can not be hurt.

This I write to brace,
To benefit and cheer
Against the coming year
Those who stand apart
Because they care for art
With sanity of mind
And charity of heart,
Of whom I know a few,
For instance, you, my dear.

How foolish of me, though!
If I know, so must you,
Being endowed with grace,
The steel within will hold
And no more lose the tunes
Than a carved sword its runes,
The steel within will hold,
The steel within will ring,
The steel within will sing
In spite of any cold,
And long before the spring.

ARIA

Music lifting and falling
Waiting itself below
The bowl at the base of the fountain

Spilling the overflow
In streams of silk and silver
To runnels underground:
The music is more like water
In pattern than in sound.

Moreover, hear this music
And see this water rise
In light almost more brilliant
Than that of Paradise,
Light beyond light, revealing
No fleck of time, no trace
Of cloud, no bar of shadow
To mark the dial's face.

The double rush and cadence
Of intricate delight,
Music lifting and falling
Like water, clear and bright,
And light, beyond all radiance,
Intense, complete, profound—
No cloud on the golden mountain,
No shade on the golden ground.

FORBID THY RAVENS

A LANDSCAPE, AND A LADY

This orchard must have been imaginary
Or in a dream's domain, not really there.
Full round, bright red, the apple and the cherry
Hung ripeness down, as if to double and share
A season out of time, and temperate air
That might have been October or July,
When apricots and grapes in color vie
With the early purple plum, and the late golden pear.

And what design would have a garden laid
So close beneath an over-arching tree?
Yet, strangely, the great maple cast no shade
Even on summer noons, and curiously
Thickened and thinned; one moment it would be
Dark-green or black as thunderstorm and doom,
And eyes would close, then open, look up, and see
Orange autumnal fire, pale yellow springtime bloom.

And who could call the season early or late?
Time, ranker than the hardy weeds, had found
An entrance through the wall or fence or gate
And overstepped his ordinary bound:
Asparagus thrust six inches from the ground,
Yet corn in tassel stood; wax-beans were curly,
Pumpkins like basketballs; and, late or early,
The green peas, gathered, made a saddle-leather
        sound.

The scene could change before the watcher knew:
Was this another garden, or the same?
Gorgeous with scarlet, yellow, royal-blue,
Where ruby-throated humming-birds took aim
At the red bee-balm; where the goldfinch came
To the golden-glow; or the rare tanager
Burned like an ember of the poppies' flame;
Where purple aster rhymed with lilac's lavender.

Yet there was winter visible in the east:
Across brown fields the tattered leaves were blowing,
And some one on a gray and jaded beast,
Cowboy or knight, there was no way of knowing
In the bewildering dusk, with daylight going,
Stumbled down-hill across the hummocked grass,
An image seen through snow behind a glass,
And even within the picture it was thickly snowing.

She turned her back upon the winter scene,
Famished and frozen, turned her head away,
Wanting, once more, the garden, bright and green,
Wanting, once more, the orchard, bright and gay:
"Stay," said the summer light and sunshine, "Stay!"
"Go," said the heart's persistent winter, "Go!"
"Oh, yes, oh, yes!" blossom and bird would say,
But ice and cold and darkness all kept saying, "No!"

She came a little closer, read the signs:
Trespassing Allowed, the notice said.
There was no angel with great wings outspread
Before the open gate, no serpent creeping
Into the rocky wall or through the vines,
And the old god with his broomstick tipped with red
First made her feel like laughing, then like weeping,
Then came an icy blast, to chill the dead,
And cloud was black again, and snow was swift and
      sweeping.

NIGHT GAME

Only bores are bored,—wrote William Saroyan—
And I was a bore, and so I went to the ball game;
But there was a pest who insisted on going with me.
I thought I could shake him if I bought one ticket,
But he must have come in on a pass. I couldn't see him,

But I knew he was there, back of third, in the row
    behind me,
His knees in my back, and his breath coming over my
    shoulder,
The loud-mouthed fool, the sickly nervous ego,
Repeating his silly questions, like a child
Or a girl at the first game ever. *Shut up,* I told him,
*For Christ's sweet sake, shut up, and watch the ball
    game.*
He didn't want to, but finally subsided,
And my attention found an outward focus,
Visible, pure, objective, inning by inning,
A well-played game, with no particular features,—
Feldman pitched well, and Ott hit a couple of homers.

And after the ninth, with the crowd in the bleachers
    thinning,
And the lights in the grandstand dimming out behind
    us,
And a full moon hung before us, over the clubhouse,
I drifted out with the crowd across the diamond,
Over the infield brown and the smooth green
    outfield,
So wonderful underfoot, so right, so perfect,
That each of us was a player for a moment,
The men my age, and the soldiers and the sailors,
Their girls, and the running kids, and the plodding
    old men,
Taking it easy, the same unhurried tempo,
In the mellow light and air, in the mild cool weather,
Moving together, moving out together,
Oh, this is good, I felt, to be part of this movement,
This mood, this music, part of the human race,
Alike and different, after the game is over,
Streaming away to the exit, and underground.

HELL

Hell is a place of solitude enforced
On the great host, cut off by sorrow, going
Under a wind intolerably cold,
A wind from no direction, always blowing.

Hell is a place of everlasting noise,
Where voices, plaintive and obnoxious, cry
Over and over again their favorite word
In constant iteration: *I, I, I*.

Hell is a place where mirrors are black water,
And rivers salt, and atmosphere like lead,
Where suffering is all the rage and fashion,
And everything is dead, except the dead.

Hell is all right to visit, if we have to,
And hard enough to miss, in any case;
But, I insist, I would not like to live there,
Not if you gave me all the God-damned place.

MAXIM

*Out of this nettle, danger, we pluck
this flower, safety.* KING HENRY IV,
PART I: ACT II, SCENE 3.

Hotspur was right, of course,
Reading his letter alone
Walking the granite flags
In Warkworth's pile of stone.

But only halfway right:
A somewhat subtler truth
Lies in the sentence, hid
From any lack-brain youth

However rash and brave,
Eluding such as he,
More meaning, deeper sense,—
Transpose the nouns, and see.

Here is what middle age
Must learn and face, aware
Of menace underground,
Of malice in the air.

Luxuriant and rank,
Choking the garden beds,
Coarse herb with stinging hair,
The nettle grows and spreads.

Yet, with soft feigning, makes
Most plausible and real
Its mimicry of down,
Of mullein, flax, all-heal.

O my lord fool, beware
The nettle in disguise,
The comforting pretense,
The dubious certainties.

Despise the milksop self,
The shallow coward hind,
With coldness in the heart,
With panic in the mind.

Disown that inner rogue
Whose apprehensive fear
Is grovelling, is base,
Is utterly sincere.

Be violent and prompt
Before the spirit sickens,
And where the clump of weeds,
Close and familiar, thickens,

Come trampling down the growth
Like a marauding stranger,
Thrust out the hand, and pluck
This bright red flower, danger.

REFLECTIONS

You hold the mirror up to Nature,
And what do you get out of that, vain creature?
You have to look sideways, and that's absurd,
And the objects are all reversed or blurred.

But a personal image might be clearer,
So you look at yourself in another mirror;
Your right arm lifts, in a kind of pass,
And a southpaw waves at you out of the glass.

And how can you trust what your eyes have seen,
When quarter of eight is four-fifteen?
So maybe the blind are the better guide,
Taking their mirrors in their stride.

Smash your mirrors, and you'll be stuck,
For seven years, with the worst of luck,
But what the adage neglects to state
Is, if you don't smash them, it might be eight.

Cases are known of persons found,
All of their life-time, caught spell-bound,
Fixed on themselves, confronting these
Smooth-faced entrancing surfaces.

Mirrors are useful enough, no doubt,
If your tie's not straight, or your shirt-tail's out,
If the edge of your slip hangs down and shows,
Or you've lip-stick smeared all over your nose.

O.K. for the smart and chi-chi bitches
Who never will know which aspect which is,
But not too reliable to employ
In a serious quest for the real McCoy.

Get out of the house; pass the mirror by
With a last quick glance from a fond vain eye,
Then, having forgotten the looking-glass,
Observe the clouds and the trees and the grass,

And the men and the women, going places,
With the sunlight falling across their faces,
Their inner light, and their darker care—
Don't worry: you'll find your image there.

As much as you want to, maybe more,
In the real and visible world, before
It's time to quit, and call it a day,
And you've not said half what you meant to say.

NARCISSA

Here every surface is forever gloss;
Even Time's smooth sliding
Is a great pier-glass for her, slowly drawn,
In panoramic gliding.

Her days are hanging mirrors, and her hours,
Like ivory-handled looking-glasses, lie
On varnished dressers, ready to the hand,
Convenient to the eye.

And even the little moments, quickly taken,
Like a compact from a pocket in a purse,
Reflect, with brief but shining reassurance,
Their offered segment of the universe.

So to the street; and oh, the city glitters
Brightly around her progress; where she treads
The avenues are sleek and supple rivers,
Along whose banks the people turn their heads.

Their heads are turned, it seems, in admiration,
And the plate-glass windows gleam
Holding, alike, her motion and her pauses,
Her fixity, her dream.

She walks below the trees, whose leaves are burnished.
Spangles of bronze or copper, and whose bark
Is polished, like a colonnade of pillars,
Black marble, on the pathways of the park.

And after these she comes to the round water,
Gun-metal color, luminous and dark,
Looks over the railings, looking at her halo,
Unbroken, in the perfect curving arc.

Beautiful world! And even more delightful,
In the secret close, to meet and recognize,
Double and pure and absolutely faithful,
Her smiling image in her lover's eyes.

A WORD OF GUIDANCE

—after V. Van Gogh

Young man, beware the cheap and easy lady
Whose charms are just a little over-blown,
Whose voice is just a shade too loud in public,
Who calls you up too often on the phone.

Dearie, she calls you, but there's nothing binding
In her caresses; you are more than free
To fool around with any other lovers,
As many as you want to; so is she.

Exciting, and promiscuous, and eager,
Her fond embrace—for she is not unkind—
Does not unduly elevate the spirit,
Nor yet, unduly, agitate the mind.

She'll give you something, flatter you, and spoil you,
Butter you up, cajole, and coax, and smile,
And wear you down, and ultimately leave you
For some slick number in the latest style.

                    *   *

And equally beware her frigid sister,
The lady with the choker made of ice,
Whose manner is a model of decorum,
Whose language is meticulously nice.

Chaste, if you call it chastity to gather
Your passion to her unresponsive breast,
Distrain your lust, and make your single ardor
The prize possession of the unpossessed.

Oh, what a horror! Succuba of plaster,
Cold to the body, sanctimonious witch,
Female with no redeeming female folly,
A viper and a vampire and a bitch.

No Circe, though she makes you less than human,
And no Medusa, though she makes you stone,
And no Calypso, any way you take her—
Why take her, anyway? Leave her alone!

                    *   *

Between the vulgar and the academic
A man would be an idiot to choose,
Nothing from one, and zero from the other:
Whichever way you figure it, you lose.

                    *   *

But wait a moment. There is still another
Whom it might be worth going far to find,
And all she asks is your entire devotion,
Body and spirit, heart and soul and mind.

And loving her involves much disillusion,
Yet agony alone does not suffice
To win her favor; that requires rejoicing,
And loving her is worth whatever price.

For she will give you love, beyond all knowing,
Exhaust you, and renew you, and restore;
And you will be surprised at understanding
Things that you never understood before.

As simple as that. Oh, yes; and she will make you
Thoughtful and strong, serene, amused, and gay:
Young man, I think you might be happy with her—
Cette dame Nature, cette dame Réalité.

RENDER UNTO CÆSAR

One side of the coin has a vicious monarch's face,—
His image and superscription written plain—
Evil and tyrannous. The other side
Has a crown of laurel, and stars, and a field of sky.

Nobody, taking the coin from purse or pocket,
Holding its weight in the hollow of the hand,
Ever wonders which side is the more important,
Which is the one that makes it legal tender.
The only question is this one, very simple:
What will the money buy?

Hard and durable metal. Centuries after
Its empire crumbles, the disk and the imprint keep
Their mark, their shape, under the ash and rubble,

Under the loam, unearthed some day, and studied,
Rubbed bright again, the tyrant and the laurel,
Placed under glass in an up-to-date museum,
Current no longer, coin of the realm no more,
Purchasing power lost, but the value greater,
Greater than any it ever had before.

THE ANGELS

Angels, within the plague-infected city,
Confront the sickly population's gaze
With neither arrogance nor too much pity,
Continue on their ways

Untroubled by the intrigues of infection
Whose barricades are built in every square,
Whose barb-wire tangles every intersection;
They pass through these like air.

Their only armor is their own completeness;
They carry no archaic sword or shield;
Their mirth is music of compelling sweetness;
Their presence, light revealed.

However black the alleys of suspicion,
However thick and pestilent the air,
They go, unscathed, unscathing, on their mission;
They heal by being there.

For they are Being's perfect revelation,
Whose very essence is Becomingness,
Intense existence, pure illumination;
They more than heal, they bless.

So, as they reach the city's edge and harbor,
And walk, across the water, out of sight,
The silence, offering music to the darkness,
Receives the gift of light.

HAWTHORNE COURT

In the young maples that line the flagstone sidewalk
Of the residential block, in the ivy that covers
The five brick stories, the sparrows are loud at day-
    break.

In the bedroom, warm, with both the windows open,
The restless sleeper stirs, the belated slumber
Broken by this obstreperousness of sparrows.

There are hundreds of sparrows, hundreds, all of a
      twitter,
Garrulous, chattering, scolding, making a racket
From sheer delight at their own incessant jabber.

We rise and dress. We do not hear the sparrows
For the sound of the water running in the bathroom,
The toilet flushing, the early morning broadcast,

The click and slam of the heavy door of the icebox,
The clatter that comes from washing the breakfast
    dishes
As the zinc receives the silver and the china.

Pillows are thumped, beds moved on jarring casters,
The dumbwaiter ends its creaking trips for garbage,
Then, for a quarter hour, there is perfect stillness.

In the living-room, all blue and green and shaded,
The Oriental poppy's big red petal
Drops to the floor, with a little sound like cardboard.

And then, halfway between sunrise and noontime,
The chattering comes again, through other windows,
On the side away from the street, louder and louder,

Louder, as if the sun were an amplifier,
And more articulate, but the same in temper,
Garrulous, shrill, the chatterers delighted,

Quarrelsome, scolding. But these are not the sparrows;
The sparrows are under the eaves and in the ivy;
These are the children playing in the garden.

NOBLESSE OBLIGE

My lord and lady, whose ancestral titles
Are, it may be, Her Grace,
And His Serene, or His Most Tranquil, Highness,
In the abundant space

Of their estate, part company for moments,
For hours. Each entertains
With separate welcome, common guests who visit
Their green and rich domains.

Each with a group, by waterfall or fountain,
Below majestic trees,
By path or pool, they stroll, converse, and gesture,
Extending courtesies.

Or seated overlooking lawn and garden,
They hear musicians play
The strings and flutes, concealed in bower or arbor,
Airy, sedate, and gay,

Haydn or Mozart. And a strain of music
Carries across the space
Between them, so that His Most Tranquil Highness
Smiles, thinking of Her Grace.

Neither unduly anxious for the other,
Along their ways they move
With a more active graciousness than patience,
Secure in wealth and love.

Patrician in their habit and composure,
Serene and sure, they know
Each guest, however fair the entertainment,
Will rise, and bow, and go,

Even those lingerers like Time and Absence
Regretfully depart,
And they may be, again, alone together,
 Discoursing, heart to heart.

COLUMBA, DATIVE AND ACCUSATIVE

The gay little girl, in the pink little dress, is running
After the pigeons, the plump little arms raised high,
The plump little fingers making a cup already,
Laughing and happy, liking the way they fly,
Laughing and happy, because she almost has one:
Maybe she means to be cruel, to chase and frighten,
Maybe she only knows they are bright, exciting,
Beautiful and alive, and she wants one so.

And across the walk in space, but in time much
       farther,
At the other end of the asphalt path of years,
The little old man, with the crumpled sack of pea-
       nuts,
Colored and shaped like his hand, is smiling, daffy,
But wise enough, in his foolishness, to know
That the thing to do with anything bright and lovely
Is to give it something, to feed it and to love it,
And let it come to the sleeve and shoulder, so.

114

LANDSCAPE, OR PORTRAIT

The leaves have hardly turned at all.
This might be August, or July,
Warm, rich, mature, emotional,

Yet just a little crisp and dry,
A little—shall we say?—subdued.
Something has gone, is going, by,

Receding. Greater quietude.
Less light. A more determined will
To curb exuberance of mood.

While richness and emotion still
Mellow decorum's proper claims,
This warmth permits a hint of chill.

Facing the park, this window frames
A masterpiece of early fall,
Perfectly done, by Henry James.

OLD MAN, MADISON SQUARE,
SEPTEMBER EVENING

Whatever work there was to do is over:
The obligations, the resentments, end.
It is good to have, at last, some hours of freedom,
Some hours of grace, to spend,

After the sun goes down, at the end of summer,
As the world swings round toward winter, spins to-
        ward dark,
To come here to this temporary station,
This little city park,

With no one to confide in but the evening,
And, for that matter, without any need
To share with any one the disappointments,
The hopes, the self; indeed,

It is good to know perception only: passion,
Experience, expression, cry no more
With various voice; and patience makes no murmur.
The arteries' rush and roar

Slows in the traffic of the island city.
It is not so bad, not now, to be alone
Watching, without anxiety, those others,
People, and trees, and stone.

Lovers draw closer, with a premonition
Of chill in the air, and lateness. In the tower
The dial tells the time with two thin shadows;
The bells announce the hour.

The leaves, with more of space and less of substance,
Make reminiscence of their summer sound
Stir for a moment, pour and pause, and loosen
The driest to the ground.

And none of this disturbs the quiet figure
With the neat gray beard, in the neat dark suit, at ease,
A good old man, observing, with composure,
People, and stone, and trees.

AUTUMNAL

Face it—you must—and do not turn away
From this bright day,
Intolerably glorious and bright,
Red-gold and blue by day, white-gold and blue by
        night.

Face it, and, doing so,
Be wise enough to know
It is Death you face, it is Death whose colors burn
Gold, bronze, vermilion in the season's turn.

But Death with honor, gay
In pomp and fine array,
In glory and pride, spectacular and bright,
Gathering, giving, light.

A pure translation, whose impermanence
Informs the watching sense
Not with despair, but memory and praise
Of the three other seasons' perfect days.

Not only all that lives, but all that dies
Is holy, having lived, and testifies
To bravery in season, spirit, man.
Face it. You must. You can.

THE DOUBTCASTER

The voice is cultured, almost—above the fashion
Of the slick studio stereotype; not unctuous,
Not quite insidious, nor ingratiating;
Intromissive, call it; and imagine
Intercourse conducted without passion,
That kind of undisturbing penetration.

And individual, beyond all question:
You can recognize it at a moment's notice,
Informed, ironical, a little mocking,
But not offensive, not overtly shocking,
Disarming by its candor, as if to say,
"We are on to ourselves, we are wise, we know the
    answers."

117

And versatile: comes on at any hour,
On any subject, over any station,
With comments on the labor situation,
Science, and politics, and modern art;
Sometimes discusses matters of the heart,
Dissuading lovers; or predicts the weather.

A curious thing—no two describe the voice
In the same terms, and yet they all agree
That something makes it different, unique,
Original. They wonder. Can it be
Its truly sympathetic character?
—*No man has really heard his own voice speak.*

Oh, very popular in the Crossley rating!
The listeners include the high-class people
Who write to QXR for program booklets,
The followers of *Information Please*
And Sunday concerts from the Friends of Music
And weekly book-chats. And not only these.

Housewives tune in in the middle of the morning;
The girl who comes to do the heavy cleaning
Tunes in; the weary husband, home again,
Over the second highball before dinner,
Tunes in. They all tune in, their favorite program.
Children, however, treat it with disdain.

Those who can't sleep at night get up to listen,
But it is heard, as well, outside the home.
You can hear it, for example, in a taxi,
When the driver drops the flag to take the fare,
Puts down his tabloid, keeps the radio going;
In bars, in lobbies, you can hear it blare.

You can hear it, now and then, at some one's party,
In a lull amid the general stir and shuffle,
When people, holding glasses, pause a while,

Break off the conversation, crowding closer,
Hushed worshippers, to kneel before the dial,
Or bow their heads above the inner circle.

And, now and then, a heretic is found
Who growls in protest, "Oh, my God!" and goes
Into another room and shuts the door,
And even so cannot escape the sound,
Its implications coming through the walls,
And wonders if he ought to listen more.

For all the time, wherever people gather,
They talk about this voice, proclaim its praise.
Most of the rest are terrible, they grant you,
But he is different, he's really good,
He makes things clear they never understood,
Gives facts, confers perception on their days.

So much they love him, people quote his phrases
Unconsciously, believing them their own,
Unconsciously appropriate his tone,
Profess, like him, a subtle disillusion,
So fond, so proud, they do not realize
Their own compulsion as they plagiarize.

So bound to him in spirit, they can never
Be happy till they see him face to face.
His autograph, his signature below
His kind responsive intimate personal letter
Is not, alas, enough. They almost falter
At their presumption, but they tell him so.

They must behold him in the holy place,
They must adore their idol at his altar,—
Could they have tickets for the studio?
Waiting is nothing, when devotion moves
The longest line along to what it loves,
And one by one, rewarded, in they go.

And each one thinks, at first, on entering there,
He is alone and looking in a mirror,
And as the image smiles and waves him nearer,
He is startled, and reflects, "How strange that he
Should look, and dress, and sound, so much like me!"
And realizes he is on the air.

But who is on the air? His own lips move,
His own heart speaks, he knows each word, he hears
His secret apprehension amplified.
Too loud, the voice reverberates and rolls,
Monstrous, immense, a roaring in his ears—
There must be something wrong with the controls.

Dreadfully wrong. The face behind the glass
Comes through the glass, but does not break the glass,
Expands, dilates enormously, is drowned,
Dissolving under overwhelming sound,
And sound, become a solid, nullifies
All space, all light. Darkness and panic rise.

Darkness and panic and the voice of doubt
Close in on him, poor little man, who tries
To grope to find the wall, to raise a shout,
But no attendant hears him when he cries
"Where is the exit?" There is no way out,
He has listened once too often, and he dies.

THE BELLS

Bells in the Sunday air
Send to the hills around
A sound, a simple sound,
Not music, only nearly,
The motes, the elements
Of music, rising clearly,
Hovering, circling there,

Beyond the measuring sense
To tell how far, how high,
The pure announcement goes.

Whatever ruin dwells
In upper atmosphere
Above the reach of bells,
Here on his hillside ground,
However lost and lonely,
The listener, who knows
The season's innocence,
And shares, with all his heart,
The innocent season's cry,
Love me, can wait and hear

After a moment only,
The beautiful reply
Across the Sunday air,
The reassuring sound,
Not music, only nearly,
Sustained, sustaining, clearly
Repeating, simply, still—
I have, I do, I will.

THE DEEP-ROOTED

The fears and the doubts
Are a wind in the boughs,
Darkening color
In the green summer,
Shaking the trees
In any season
With a rush of terror
Loud in the air.

But no sound rages
Under the ground

Where the roots take hold
Going down, going deep,
Going wide as the crest
In the upper air:
No wind blows there
Of doubt or fear.

So they are nourished,
Abide, abound,
Taking the changes
Of heat and cold:
Blossom in spring;
Ripen in summer;
Yield in the fall;
In winter, wait.

So they are great;
So they are tall;
So they produce
In rich profusion
More than a harvest,
Even in darkness
When the wind rises,
Making of storm
Dancing and music
Imposing, always,
On all disorder
Design and form.

OAK AND LINDEN

This opulence of lawn and shade,
Lavish, luxuriant, and dark,
With copious green donation grows,
Promoting suburb into park,

And, rich in false assumption, proves
That summer is most real and long

Of all the times and seasons. This,
Unhappily, we know, is wrong.

Discounting transient spring and fall,
We wait for what we always knew
Was ultimate,—winter, withering,
Bitterness. Nothing else was true.

Endearments, like the fading days,
With every repetition pale,
Lose warmth. The amulets are lost;
The properties of magic fail.

Not always. Some, whose wisdom goes
Beyond our cautious wit, can share
Their substance, even with strangers; give
To gods, unknown, their daily fare,

And, having loved each other long,
Gain, late in life, their due reward;
Behold the humble house become
Marble and gold, for them to guard;

Promised, besides, that neither one
Shall ever see the other's tomb,
Philemon, Baucis, end their days
As double towers of shade and bloom.

CONCERTO IN D MAJOR

All the contending elements of music
Under the urging of the hand and mind
Keep pace, respond, along their guided courses,
Vie for position—sinew, frame, and wind.

With common aim, yet each against the other,
And each one with the other, so they strive,

One dominant, one fading for the moment,
And all so beautiful, and so alive,

Making their varied restlessness and rushing,
Their separate color and movement, pause and pace,
Compose, from rival multiple divergence,
One harmony, one unity, one grace.

So, all together. And the pattern swiftly
Breaks into change. The single melody,
Released, leaps forth in bright determination,
Beyond the others, running clear and free.

And all of this is only heard, but, hearing,
I more than hear the music. I am shown—
O double gift of sound—its very image
Made visible in racing flesh and bone,

And I am in the stands again, and happy,
Watching the field swing round the turn, and see
One coming on, ahead of all contention,
Beyond the others, running clear and free,

The bright silks shining in the air like music,
The rush of music closing like the wind,
The full crescendo surging to the finish
Under the urging of the hand and mind.

SCALES AND SCORPION

All of the coarse late-blooming summer flowers,
Whose license ought to end with any frost,
Indulged beyond their actuarial hours,
Luxuriate, hysterical almost,
When the warm wind blows over them at noon,
Effusive in exaggerated praise
Of this absurd extension of their days.

Old blowsy dahlias, saffron and maroon,
Outface the poor but honest calendar;
The cannas flounce, in ostentatious boast,
Their dowdy reds and yellows; and the rose,
Whose blush is now magenta, coyly lays
Her check against the scaly trellis bar:
And a warm wind in mid-October blows,—

A humid, warm, anachronistic wind,
Condensing, in the temper of the mind,
Too many sultry sullen summer moods,
Black thunder-clouds, and dark and ominous woods,
Too much of restiveness, too little rest,
Too much of south, too little north and west,
And far too much reluctance in the breast.

Who, in such weather, cares to look beyond
The moment, false and fatuous and fond?
Who can admit the bitter truth we hate,
Winter's oncoming, cold and desolate?
Who feels enough conviction of despair
To lift his voice with honesty, and cry,
"So little time is left before decay!"?

So little time is left. But anyway,
Who would believe it? Neither you nor I,
Breathing this heavy sentimental air,
While this excessive summer lingers on,
Like a big slattern, spoiled and overgrown,
In sheer ill-nature, bold and obstinate,
When common decency would have her gone.

TACENT SATIS LAUDANT

In the still and airless night
Sounds carry as over water
And when they are heard no longer

Or even imagined heard
You can feel the depths of silence
Resuming their poise again
In the way that water would
Were it broken and stirred
And roiled, and slowly then
Cleared and closed over,
All interruption lost,
Absorbed, absolved forever
In air more dense than air,
Lost in the mist, or gone
Down like a sunken stone.

THE OAK LEAF

At November's weary end, oh, late November,
   I was walking along the street,
Eyes on the ground, and noticed a brown something
   Almost under my feet.

An oak leaf, ragged and dry like tattered leather,
   Was what I thought I saw,
But it changed before my eyes. It was flesh, and living,
   A little brown hand or claw.

Thrust up, as it were, from underneath the pavement,
   Held out for alms, before it had to go
Pulled down by the unseen arm to the airless darkness
   At the will of the man below.

This was a test. I knew it, and I feared it.
   I was afraid, but I could understand
I must not stoop to put my copper pennies,
   Or the ones that looked like silver, in that hand.

126

I had done this many times before, too often;
    I knew I must never again
Degrade myself with pity, or think for a moment
    I was better off than any other men,

Whatever the element of airless darkness
    In which they breathed, through which their utter
        need
Thrust up the shrivelled hand, the claw, the talon
    Too brown and dry to bleed.

And as I looked, it changed, a hand no longer,
    But a copper-colored gauntlet, or a glove,
Flung in another kind of test, a challenge
    Hurled at me from above.

And I knew who flung the gauntlet, winter, winter,
    The skinny bully, mean and cold and grim,
With no red-blooded martial heart, but itching
    To make me fight with him.

Another test. If I took this dare, bent over,
    Picked up this glove, and recognized this foe,
I would make myself his size, or a little smaller;
    Oh no, I said, oh no.

I have been through this before, I know this phony,
    His every ruse and gambit, his hateful ways
Infecting me with love and admiration
    Till I detested even April days.

Not any more. I laughed. What was there, really,
    Except a tattered oak leaf lying there
Before my feet, fallen before its season
    Through the November air?

I set my foot upon it, heard it crackle,
    And almost heard its poor thin little cry,

And I raised my eyes, and saw, at the tips of the
  branches,
The buds against the sky.

RHONABWY'S DREAM

Owain ap Urien,
Prince of Rheged,
Bade his banner
Be raised again;
Rallied his ravens,
Thrice a hundred,
A black bane
To Arthur's army.

Owain and Arthur
Studied each other
Over the chess-board
Made all of silver.
"Owain," said Arthur,
"Forbid thy ravens."
"Play thy game, Lord!"
Said Owain.

The wingèd warriors
Far from forbidden
By that banner
Rose up, wrathful;
Tumult and triumph
Took them and tossed them,
Fierce in their fury
From hurt and pain.

Over the chess-board
Owain and Arthur,
Poring, marvelled,
Paused and hearkened.

"Owain," said Arthur,
"Forbid thy ravens."
"Play thy game, Lord!"
Said Owain.

The weather darkened.
To Arthur's side
A knight came riding,
All flame and scarlet,
Whose lance, blue-shafted,
From point to haft
Was darker dyed
With blood and plumage.

"Carest thou not,
O king," he cried,
"For thy young men slain,
For thy household's damage?"
"Owain," said Arthur,
"Forbid thy ravens."
"Play thy game, Lord!"
Said Owain.

From the board of silver,
Very slowly,
With thumb and finger
Arthur lifted
One golden bishop.
In Arthur's fist
The golden bishop
Crumbled to dust.

Then Owain beckoned
His younger brother,
A prince of Rheged,
Giving the order
To have his banner
Lowered again.
So it was lowered,
And peace did reign.

THE WIND OF TIME

LITTLE FUGUE

Wind running over the reeds like water
Reeds like sea-weed under the wind
Bending and rising, under and over—
So, in the wind of Time, the mind
Seems to bow and recover
Under the run of the river.

Like running water over the reeds
Wind is pouring its weight of air:
The way of Time, like a stream,
With rush and rest proceeds,
A rush, and a rest, and a stir,
And moods are water-weeds.

The bend and the rise, the rest and the rush,
The rush and the reed, and the wind running over,
The weigh and the wait of Time
Under the run of the water
Pouring forever—hush!—
Forever and ever and ever.

THE ISLANDS

The stars, in dissolution burning,
Burn out, as we do, late or soon,
Islands of fire, the fixed, the turning,
Whose morning and whose afternoon
Are half a trillion years, a span
As brief, or long, as his for man.

My son, when dark comes down, comes down
To the south lawn to study these:
Knowing from books the proper noun

133

For what, to me, are mysteries,
He finds the one he looks for, there,
Above the apple-tree, Altair.

Altair in August. April gone
Four months—or is it only hours?—
Since, resting on the same south lawn,
I lay and looked at yellow flowers
Moving a little when the wind
Came round the corner; and the mind

Stirred, also, idly, wondering
How long the flower had been in bloom,
How many days were left, this spring,
Before its withering and doom;
How long before it had to die
It could not tell. No more could I.

One, two, three, four; infinities,
Or moments? daffodil or man?
It would be best to look at these
O most intensely, while you can,
My trouble said, my wisdom knew,
Who knows? another year or two . . .

But no such worry seems to scare
And no self-conscious panic stir
My summer student of Altair,
Sixteen-year-old astronomer,
Taking it easy; it appears
The stars, and he, have years and years.

One, two, three, four; four, three, two, one,
Less than immortal, burning out,
Father and flower, star and son,
And only one assailed by doubt,
Daffodil, boy, and man, and star,
Most separate, most insular.

WILLOW GROVE

Still the dissembling music floats,
Corrupt, deciduous, and gay.
The leaves come down like notes, the notes
Like leaves; the players put away

Their racks and instruments; they hurry,
Faster than usual; the park,
For once, lacks dawdlers; people worry;
The air is prematurely dark.

Dark, and a storm may come. The wind
Lifts for a moment, sweeps the square
Of litter, leaves, and leaflets, thinned
By the low rush of restless air.

While one, reluctant, from his scene
Of triumph, snaps his case, and goes
Down the brief stair, across the green,
Unhappy at the season's close.

But even he, at last, is gone,
By his own sorrow overtaken.
Frail island in a desert lawn,
The ugly kiosk stands, forsaken.

Light, coming quickly under the cloud,
Slants bright, illumining, too late,
A golden shrine behind a crowd
Bent for the outer iron gate,

Nervous, intent, beyond recall,
Gone, now, too far to hear again
The final drops of music fall
With the first single notes of rain.

THE JADED

They have come from far; they have come from very
    far,
And they are wearier than they are wise.
Their manliness is spent; their cheekbones are
Hollow below their old beleaguered eyes
Which seek, once more, the cities of the plain
With dubious nostalgia, and in vain.

Listening, they have seen confusion darken,
And, watching, they have heard disaster sound;
They do not, any longer, care to hearken
To oracles and prophets, having found
Belief a stimulus, which made them strong
For a few moments, never very long.

And now their will is tenuous as smoke
Or veils of mist from vales of mist arising;
Their courage, thin as any beggar's cloak,
Shrinks from advice, and shudders at advising;
Sun is no less endurable than rain;
Both laurels and forget-me-nots are vain.

Gray mountains rise before them, whence they hear
No water, only wind across the rock,
And time, their one attraction, draws them near
To space where time is measured by no clock,
To boundaries beyond the power of song
To stir them, by its brevity, for long.

THE MANTLE

—at Venus obscuro gradientes aere saepsit.

It was no goddess cast that cloud around you,
Dark air where'er you walk, and veils of mist

Lest any sight or sound or touch confound you,
Or question halt you, devious egoist.

Never the golden Cyprian, the mover
Of all that moves along the shores of light
Caused this unreal, untoward pall to cover
The world's external substance, rich and bright.

No: your own little trinity of error,
Self-love, self-praise, and self-deception drew
The triple cloud, to serve alike for mirror,
For shield and sounding-board, to comfort you.

Rapt in that cloud, your sense can not distinguish
Subject from object, can not recognize
The echo of its own disgust or anguish;
Always, it seems, an oracle replies.

Always an oracle, whose inspiration
Confers enlightenment, a silver glow,
A golden rain, a false illumination
Within the shrouded compass where you go

Directionless and limited and stalking
In your own phantom company, a vain
And solitary host, forever walking
The boundaries of that immense terrain,

Your self . . . The sun, hot to its noon ascending,
Burns off the cloud; the shrinking veil is thinned
To wisp of fog, to rag, to nothing, ending
The gray pretense. By afternoon the wind

Blows fresh, revealing what? A sorry figure
Fearful of night, the chill, the misery
Of homelessness, a dissipated beggar
Shambling between the sea-wall and the sea.

Or, in another light, another creature,
A monstrous baby, whom no mother hears
Bawling, its rage distending every feature,
Red in the face, soiled with its dirty tears.

So it was all so useless, that assumption
Of solemn murk, layer on layer, fold
On thickening fold, bestowing no exemption
From hunger, nakedness, exposure, cold.

Better, protected from, not by, the darkness,
If one must wear a cloak, to have it shine
In color like the garment worn by Martin,
Double when halved, redder than blood or wine,

And warm not only with its own astounding
Richness of substance, scarlet thread and weave,
But from its owner's heart, in love abounding.
O my poor mendicant, for once, believe!

THE STATUE

Short, husky, black and brown with dust and sweat
The quarry men, whose bar and sledge have pried
The marble loose, stand back to watch it drawn
Down the rough skidroad from the mountainside,

Out of its first exposure, heading toward
A new erosion, where a mind, an eye,
And something called imagination, wait
To wear it down, before the hands dare try

To grasp and lift the chisel and the maul,
One man's complete employment now,—observe
How stone is dressed in nakedness, how steel
With sharp straight edge brings out the bevelled curve.

One man does this, who stops at times, and frowns,
Or hums himself a little tune that goes,
When all goes well, *The more the marble wastes,*
The more it wastes, the more the statue grows.

Finished, at last (he thinks) and sold, and set
In some appropriate spot, a colonnade
Or Syracusan grove, where oranges
Are balls of sun among the globes of shade.

Here, like its owner's fortune, just a trace
Too new for dignity, the statue stands,
Almost a masterpiece, requiring still
Some final touch, the work of other hands.

And these are given; wind and rain and sun,
Time and the weather, infinitely slow,
Patient through generations, waste and wear,
Correct the marble, make the figure grow,

So that tradition, anciency, and grace
Are added by subtraction, and the pure
Symbol from image forms, along whose base
Runs the new rune—*See how our works endure.*

Endure, disintegrate, and, even beyond
Disintegration, live in long renown:
After the vandals come, lop off the limbs,
Hack at the head and helmet, topple down

The mutilated torso, drag it off
Aboard a ship, to cast it in the seas,
Granted its last perfection, men recall
Its glory in one word—Praxiteles.

TEST PAPER

What do we praise?—Sunsets, and open fires,
America, and mother love, I guess;
The merry laughter of a little child,
And poems that touch the heart with tenderness.

What do we really praise?—Oh, Life and Time,
(With capitals), books that Fadiman commends,
The chromium bars, the streamlined cars and trains,
The music played for music's newest friends.

What do we praise beyond all this?—High art
God's majesty and sacraments and grace,
The universal music of the spheres,
The mysteries of interstellar space.

Come down to earth. What is it you and I,
My love, deep in our heart of hearts, adore,
Cherish, and tend?—Each other. Not so fast.
Maybe, a little; but ourselves much more.

Last question. (On your honor.) What do all
Praise, absolutely, in this day and age?
Re-read the question; answer thoughtfully;
Write nothing on this portion of the page.

THE OBDURATE

—Whatever you clutch,
It is not much.
Unclench the hand,
Let go the straw,
I say, let go;
Subside, sink down,
Go under, drown.

Let the full tide
More deep than doubt
Flood in, wash out
The scribbled sand.
Abandon pride.
Surrender; cease
To pit the will
Against the word
Oblivion.
Therein alone
Is final peace.
Forget, forget;
Resign; be still.

—Some day, O Lord,
Some day. Not yet.

CONTEMPORARY ARTIST

for Robert Motherwell

I am lonely: this, at least, I surely know.
I am important: this I must believe
With neither Church nor State to tell me so.
What can I do but hate, unless I grieve?

Given no myth, no symbol, never drawn
On any great crusade or lofty quest,
My occupation, like Othello's, gone,
My talent uninvited and repressed,

Where can I turn save inward and away
From all the time's corrupting platitudes,
Whose lackeys flatter, whose assassins lay
Their ambuscades in obsolescent woods?

Where can I turn save toward the self, to find
The body and blood, the bread and wine I crave,

The grace of reassurance for the mind,
The absolute injunction to be brave?

Men lie, and things are lied about. I must
Abstract myself from these, and for defense
Against them, put my confidence and trust
In what I have of passion and of sense,

And what I have of craft,—more ways than one
To skin a cat, or keep from telling lies.
One theme recurs, when all is said and done,
Beauty is Truth, in whatsoever guise,

Truth being always, "This is how I feel,"
And never, "This is how it is—rejoice!"
Wie sagt das sich? Gar ohne Zweck and Ziel?
Objectiveless? Not quite. Perhaps by choice,

More likely by determination, I,
Given an order, go along with those
Who fight disintegration till they die,
And, without much composure, still compose.

THE DIVORCE

Light, of two elements the unison,
Of air and fire, where one and one are one,
Performs the office of division,

Enacts that earth from water sunder, sever,
Keeping their separate properties forever,
Hill, valley, mountain; ocean, lake, and river.

To each its own identity and sign,
Texture and color, boundary and line,
Motion and rest, the lift, the flow, the shine,

The melody, magnificence and mirth
All more intense, all given brighter worth
By this divorce of water and of earth.

O friends and witnesses, rejoice, approve
The single happiness in which they move;
Give them your fondest blessing, and your love.

What one made two, nothing will render one:
Darkness will overrule my lord the sun,
Darkness, annulment and negation,

The sable reconciler, who remembers
The vain petitions of unending numbers,
Brings them together in his solemn chambers.

THE DELIVERANCE

So fails the music, falls the screen of marble
Between the world and me, dissolving, broken.
The normal quarrel
Breaks out again, speaks, and is spoken.

Abroad, at home,
I smell corruption under every stone,
Touch the infected, stoop, examine dung,
And taste my own bad breath upon my tongue.

While always at my side
Stalks my official and officious guide,
A vertical nervous brown-and-yellow shadow
Forever at my elbow.

No matter. There's an old red book that tells
How, having mastered seven certain spells,
And met with many perils, one can find
The power within the mind

143

To transform objects, facing unafraid
The Half-Slim Champion, and the Loathly Lady.
The Dangerous Well, the Triple-Headed Bear
Are not so much to fear.

With time and trouble, pains and patience, learn
The lore of counter-charm. Face East and West,
And North and South, three times. Crush vervain.
   Burn
Hazel and rowan. Test

The wind's direction. Gather in the night
St. John's Wort, and All-heal.
Reach in a brook till thumb and fingers feel
A pair of perfect pebbles, round and white.

Strip yourself mother-naked; bathe in milk.
Summon a princess-royal, who will throw
Her arms around you, open her gown of silk,
And give you her green mantle when you go.

Practice at being lion, red-hot bar
Of iron, adder, esk. And then there are,
Of course, more than a few
Other and necessary things to do.

Still, if a man is brave enough and wise
To swear himself his destiny, he can
Be something more than man,
Transform himself as well as objects, rise

To be an eagle, or the blade of a sword,
A drop in the air, a boat at sea, a word
In an illumined book, a bridge, the foam
Of the wave, or the string of a harp, and come

So, through his nine fulfillments, to a grove
Where charming people, with delightful words,

144

Converse, and rest, and move
Among the blue and yellow flowers and scarlet birds,

To hear, once more, the music, hear once more
The music, find the screen no longer screen,
And all reality more bright, more clean,
Than ever it was, or could have been, before.

FIN DE SIECLE

All that I wander through, so bright, so modern,
So quick with novelty, so very wise,
So *dernier cri,* so *ne plus ultra,* this,
All this, all this, I come to realize,
All of a sudden, is not mine at all,
Is not my Now, but some one else's Then.
There will be other women, other men,
Appropriating this, still bright, but small,
Garish and glazed, of colored post-card size,
So little that it goes from hand to hand
For the delight of those who know and praise
Our customs, our *décor* and these our days:
"How irresistible! How charming!" so
Runs their gay comment on their long ago.
Secure, and, what is even better, *chic,*
These lovers of the chromium antique
Will pride themselves because they understand.

Forgive their trespasses. If we resent
Being considered quaint and innocent,
Remember—they will know, beyond a doubt,
How all the things that frightened us came out,
And, for their own anxieties, will cast
The light of certainty around the past,
Impute to others what they dare not claim,
The opposite of sorrow, guilt, and shame,

145

And even when most dubious will know
One more advantage, which might possibly
Conduce to smugness. They will surely be,
Past any contradiction, still alive
In Nineteen ninety three, and four, and five.

OF MICTURITION: A MORALITY

—from Daniel George's *Anatomy of Woe.*

Dr. T. Goodwin
Around 1680
Was somewhat inclined
To whymsicall moments.
Once, in a frolick,
He pist in the pocket
Of old Mr. Lothian—
How, never mind.

And a man from Siena
Wouldn't pass water,
Afraid he would drown,
So he said, the whole town;
So they sent for physitians,
Rang the bells backward
And they all shouted "Fire!"
This effected a cure.

The moral, if any,
Would seem to be this:
It is better to piss,
Or do anything else,
In a light-hearted way
Than to summon the solemn
And ring all the bells
And turn the town frantic:
—Sing High-ho, the antic;
Heigh-ho, the gay.

VADE MECUM

One evil action every day
Will keep psychiatrists away.
Deliberate misconduct, planned
With proper prudence, understand,
Is what it takes to do the trick
And keep the soul from getting sick.
Tenants, no more, of Paradise,
What are we,—angels, men, or mice?
Knowing the facts of life, the sin
Adherent from our origin,
Better to face our nature, sure
We can not be completely pure,
Better to cultivate our garden
Than bend the knee and sue for pardon.
This side of Hell, the apple tree
Affords convenient therapy.
Don't bite off more than you can chew,
But give Beelzebub his due.
I am no advocate, of course,
Of statutory rape, or worse,
Barratry, bigamy, or arson,
Or beating up the nearest parson,
Embracery, or fraud, or theft,
Or driving madly on the left:
No, no; no need to go so far,
Being the creatures that we are,
Any man's heart suggests at once
A million million nasty stunts
On which his turpitude can draw
Within the letter of the law.
Give up the effort, vain and wrong,
Of being noble, all day long,
Of straining, in a hopeless tussle,
Your every moral nerve and muscle.
Relax; and once a day, at least,
Contrive to be a perfect beast,
Free, uninhibited, untamed,

Unscrupulous, and unashamed,
In short, a normal man or woman,
Instead of something superhuman.
So, when the evening prayer is said,
The light turned out, and you in bed,
A healthy conscience, all night through,
Will sleep the clock around with you.

LULLABY

Somber, for thy slumber's use,
Somber and fuliginous
Be thy quilt and pillow. Quiet.
Close the eyes to all that white
Harsh, insistent, burning, mordant
Acrimony of the sun.
Nebulous oblivion
Be thy music, undiscordant,
Be thy mute obedient servant.
Let the debt survive the dun;
Never mind; go under so,
While in circles, round and round,
Wheel the silenced arcs of sound,
Moving, in their grooveless ways,
Through the antidote of days,
Infinitely smooth and slow.

ARBOR SONG

The vine on the trellis
Weaves under and over,
Under and over, weaves,
Over and under—

To the constant frame the ever inconstant wonder,
Looseness of leaves
And cling of the tendril twining,
O intricate! O rare!
Even space, even air,
Part of the order and becomingness,
Blossom as grace-note, all,
Whether moving or still,
So perfectly designed
That the sight is the sound,
No more and no less,
Beautiful, musical.

BIRD SONG

Under green
I have seen
A girl below a linden tree

Chicory
Tall as she
All along a summer lane

Color clear
Quick and pure
And a silver-age refrain

Vidi
Viridi
Phyllida sub tilia

AFTER AUSONIUS

—quis color ille vadis . . .

What color are the shallows, now that evening
Moves the late shadows forward, and the river
Is dyed with the green mountain? All the ridges
Swim in the ripple of motion, and the vine
Trembles, and is not there, and under water
Its cluster, seen through glass, is magnified.

EXCELLENTLY BRIGHT

Quicker than hazel wand
The moon discovers water
Lifts it from underground
Running or still
To stir in the light wind
All quicksilver.

All that brightness
Loosed from the hold
Of ground and of shadow
Lovers and angels praise,
Silver and running gold,
Holy, holy, holy.

THE LATE SUMMER

Everything still, oh, absolutely still.
Who would have thought Pomona was like this,
So almost like Medusa? But she is.
No breath whatever stirs
This warm domain of hers.

1 5 0

Under the drooping willows, whose festoons
Hang down like chains of green and heavy stones
Two lovers stand, holding each other close.
They neither move nor whisper; and their pose,
The taller one unbending for the kiss,
Is like the deaf, the rigid, like all those
Most hopeless listeners
Locked, shut, held fast, in nothing.

                        By the cove
The great log with the broken antler lies
Heavy and huge and gray,
An old, old ram, or mountain sheep, who came
To drink, and failed, the water being steel.

Oh, goddess, goddess, need it be this way?
Break, lift, the trance, the spell. Let the wind rise,
Let branches, in the bright September, move,
And garments flutter, as the singing girls
Take home the harvest in the cool of love.

EQUINOX

Daylight or darkness, what you hear
Along about this time of year
Is, mostly, vague and feverish whir,

September's nervous idiom—
Brief rest, reiterated hum:
Little enough is left of summer.

Cicadas, katydids keep on;
The blades revolve across the lawn
For the last time, or last but one.

151

The knives are duller, but the sense,
Sharpened by an intransigence,
Insistent rather than intense,

Feels heat subside to warmth, and light
Draw in before its opposite,
Feels terror in the temperate.

VAE VICTIS

The Romans have invaded us again,—
That decadent nation, with the melancholy
Under the ostentation and the bronze,
Misgivers, dressed in attitudes of scorn,
Corrupted by their own imposing folly,
The bands and banners, cruelty and games,
Victorious over green battalions,
Summer's luxurious easy army slain.

They line our highways, confiscate our corn,
Possess our fields and set our woods in flames.
Each year they come, each year they flash and shine,
Proud in imperial purple, orange, gold,
Maroon, magenta, madder, carmine, wine,
Vermilion, umber; arrogant and bold.

Each year, some morning finds them driven forth
In panic by a rumor from the north,
Their camps forsaken, flying for their lives
Before the keen barbarians, armed with knives,
The fierce and terrible Scythians, whose breath
Sets in the crimson vein the blue of death.

Alarm, alarm! The fires burn black by dawn,
The wavering legions vanish and are gone,
Leaving no monument, no trace to mark

The mutinous disorder in the dark
Except the hue of blood, the deep red stain
Where some courageous officer was slain,
Or, it may be, a cloak of scarlet, found
Under a maple, on the frozen ground.

AFTER THE ICE-STORM

After the ice-storm, bundled in coat and muffler,
And putting my feet down cautiously and slow,
I turned aside for a broken branch of poplar
Fallen across the snow.

Out in the street, where the branch was twig,
    I noticed
Something I had to stop for, look at twice,
A long green bud, enlarged in brittle crystal,
Encased and sheathed in ice.

Of course I knew the buds were there in winter,
But my poor observation had not seen
When I looked up at them on other mornings
How far along, how green,

How almost leaf they were, in February!
I broke the twig, and held it in my glove,
Rebuke to carelessness, to study closer,
To learn from, and to love,

To feel the least bit sentimental over,
Knowing that now it could not ever be
Fulfilled, in April, in the way of nature,
High on the poplar tree.

Too bad; but still, except for this disaster,
The single bud, so dear, so precious now,

Would have been lost with all the host of others
Above me on the bough.

Well: there was nothing I could do about it,
Except remember it, if so inclined.
I let it drop, went on where I was going,
Dismissed it from my mind.

Or did I? Frozen bud, and promise broken,
And green caught fast in ice, are, it would seem,
Matters not so conveniently forgotten.
I dreamed, and in the dream

There was warm weather, sun on land and water,
I wore my summer clothes, my arms were brown,
And I was in a boat, and going slowly
And idly looking down

Through glass, through green, through emerald
          translucence,
And far below, deep as a tree is high,
I saw the shoots of life, a shoal of fishes,
Little as buds, go by.

Little as buds, and shaped like buds, but orange,
Golden; not green, not ice-locked; darting bright,
Flashes of fire, whose element was water,
Almost too swift for sight.

My boat moved on, drawn by no sail, no rower.
What was I over now? A great white stone
Huge as a sunken iceberg, shapeless, looming
Fathoms below the known.

Not ice, not stone, not shapeless, but a goddess,
Most grave, most noble, dweller in the seas,
Majestic in her robes of marble, holding
A zither on her knees.

And there was music coming from the ocean,
Benevolent, melodious, profound,
And I heard all that lay below the surface
In that Aeolian sound.

Remember, oh remember, said the music
To wind and air and water-weed and wave,
And to my heart, *Remember, oh remember
The vows that summer gave.*

And will renew, I knew, of early morning,
Of poplar branches trembling in the night,
Fragrance, and warmth; a girl, and mirth, and
    gardens,
All marvel, all delight.

My boat had grounded on the shoals of waking,
And I, through whipping sedge and driving sand,
Trudged, when I did not stumble, toward the bar-
    ren,
The gray, the frozen land,

Willing to face, but not entirely willing
The ordinary moments of the day;
Farewell, I kept on saying to the music,
And woke, and it was May.

THE DISCOVERY

"A unicorn!" they cried, "A unicorn!"
And all came running. Noble and austere,
He took their stare, their curious gaze, and morning
Ran through their veins like cooler fire, like air
All green with earliness. No purer white
Ever in any snow by moonlight shone,
An absolute and incandescent brightness

155

From hoof to horn. A thousand flowers were fire
Around him where he halted, flesh and bone,
Survivor of the cast of any spear.

Forsaking all the ardor of the hunt,
They were content with watching him. He stood
Below the red and golden fruit, confronting
Their stir, their daze, with majesty. The shade
Was light, subdued, and there was music here
Like bloom, or light, or running stream of sound
Moving the darker leaves beyond the clearing.
Mild as the air they breathed, their quietude
Reflecting his, benign, at ease, they found
Themselves, and they were happy. This was good.

THE OFFERING OF THE HEART

Tapestry from Arras, XV Century

Against a somber background, blue as midnight,
More blank and dark than cloud, as black as storm,
The almost moving leaves are almost golden,
The light is almost warm.

Seated, a lady, wearing a cloak with ermine
Holds on her hand, correctly gloved and bent,
A falcon, without feathered hood or jesses;
Her gaze appears intent

On what her hound, good little dog, is doing
Around her ankles, left front paw in air,
Regardless of the three white careless rabbits—
He does not see them there,

Or turn, as does the falcon, toward the gallant,
The gentleman, more elegant than smart,
Who comes, in crimson cloak with ermine lining,
And offers her a heart,

156

Holding it, chastely, between thumb and finger
Whose U it does not fill, a plum in size,
A somewhat faded strawberry in color—
She does not raise her eyes.

How can a heart be beating in the bosom,
And yet held up, so tiny, in the hand?
Innocence; mystery: an Age of Science
Would hardly understand.

THE PANGS

*—atque ea nimirum quaecumque
Acheronte profundo prodita sunt
esse, in vita sunt omnia nobis.*

The stone of Sisyphus
Explodes into design;
The water, through the sieve,
Descends in purest line;
And who would think that birds
As huge, as gaunt, as these,
Could open beaks to sing
Such lovely melodies?

The thirst, the hunger, take
Sustenance from the sight
Of water, out of reach,
And apples, red and bright;
The wheel's revolving hum
Diminishes; unbound,
A happy giant strides
Across the springy ground.

All that we thought was Hell,
And we therein, forsooth,
Proves, as Lucretius showed,
The converse of the truth:

157

Hell was in us, not we
In Hell; we made it so,
Guilty self-punishers,
Who bade the cancer grow.

All nonsense: cut it out,
The wound heals over; see
Water and wheel and rock
And fruit and bird and tree
All separate, all met,
Dear love, dear world, in one
Recovered image, bright
And glorious with sun.

THE PRESENCE

—esse est percipi, aut percipere.

Under the unexisting trees, the unexisting
Drift, waver, vague as water, to and fro;
Mist under mist, and shadow under shadow,
Unoccupied, they go.

They do not see the trees, which, therefore, are not,—
Dissolved, abolished, melted into air,
The trunk, the bark, the branch, the leaf, the swaying,
So there is nothing there.

Nothing, and no one. For the unperceiving,
All those who move about and never see,
If we believe more than a part of Berkley,
Can not be said to be.

The trees are safe, however. Wait, and harken!
Perceivers are approaching, in whose tread
Comes quickness out of dark, music from shadow,
A stirring overhead,

Light almost audible, and color proving,
Past all denial, what our instinct knew,
An absolute, immune to disillusion,
The physical is true.

And even were there no one there to see it,
There would be One, a grace, a consciousness,
The seer, unseen, who comprehends, completely,
Who says, forever, *Yes*.

THE GOLDEN BIRD

THE GOLDEN BIRD

The light, refracted from the silver windows,
Crosses the street, pours through the single leaf
Left on the little maple, purest yellow,
Is focussed there, alchemical and brief.

The golden bird is a common English sparrow,
But under that leaf, and in that light, he burns
All fire, within, without, his eye a jewel,
His feathers metal, flashing when he turns.

A common bird. He will be here all winter;
You will see him, any morning, in the snow,
The color and shape of a lump of mud, or horse-dung,
And he has no song. You would not believe it, though,

Seeing him now, illumined, almost music,
So that what the eye beholds, the slower ear
Expects, at any moment, golden color
Made sound, the melody double, rich and clear.

SONG

Stir in the shifting air,
Pause, waver; let there be
Motion and rest and sound
As delicate and frail
As wind across the ground

As leaf detached from tree
Taking along the wind
The unsubstantial trail
No falconer can find
No fathomer can hear.

RITORNELLO

Whenever the theme recurs
It always varies a little:
Oboe, flauto, tromba
And the single violin
Against the bank of the strings
And the double harpsicord.
Concertare, meaning,
If my Latin is halfway right,
To strive together, to fight—
What pleasant argument
Between the four and the many,
The loud and the soft contending,
Answering, responding,
And neither side insistent,
Never an instrument
With repetition rude:
Whenever the theme recurs,
It is always a little varied,
And no more personal
Nor vehicle of mood
Than mathematics are,
Five, four, one, four, two,
Four, one, two, four, one,
A hint of infinitude
In the infinitesimal,
All order, all design,
And design with ardor moving
The ripple against the current,
The ripple along and over
The full deep-running stream,
Motion and sound recurrent
In the variable theme.

SONG FOR THE LOW VOICE

Darken, air; and mood, surrender
Under autumn's heavier languor.
Mist and murk and lassitude
Darken air; surrender, mood.

Summer shadow, summer shade
Leave the thinning tree and bough,
Gathering in thicker cloud.
Mood, surrender; darken, air.

Sultry weather turns to somber,
Chill October, warm December,
All oppressive, all obscure.
Mood, surrender; darken, air.

SHADY SONG

(from a theme by Sacheverell Sitwell)

The shadow of the mandolin
Reminds us of Olivia
Who is also shadow now,
Gone away, gone away.

Of the shepherd kings whose wands,
Broken, lean against the wall
Only ivory bones are all
That is left of ebon hands.

Hunters, hunted, both pursue
Shadows, absence: bone and shade
Linger for a little spell
Telling where their course had been.

DON QUIXOTE'S SONG

Lady, where there is music
There cannot be any evil,
And where there is light and brightness
Evil cannot avail.

Under the overcast
Or into the heart of the darkness
With taper and candle move
The penitents of light.

And the penitents of sound
Accompany their round,
Playing and singing along
The long processional.

Good confraternities
In the world's wickedness
In the cold old winter sorrow,—
Lady, their word is love.

THE KING OF THE GROVE

I

From his first victory, he had always known
The fatal challenger, some time, would break
Out of the chestnut grove that overhung
The melancholy and sequestered lake
With naked sword, aggressive, strong and young.
He knew. He had, himself, been such a one.

II

He could foresee that duel, which would be
The end of all that daytime prowling, all
That broken sleep when leaf or branch would stir

At dead of night. The priest, the murderer,
Sword in his throat, a murdered priest, would fall.
Such was the rule. He faced it willingly

III

And facing it, faced many, whom he slew
At noon, or dusk, or in the dark. The sly,
The bold, the fierce, the cunning, fell, their blood
On sand or fallen leaves. He watched them die,
Taken in rush, in ruse. So far, so good.
But his own time was coming. This he knew.

IV

Holding no barren argument with pride,
He knew his arm, his eye, his craft, his will
Were failing, that a hundred other men
Could equal or surpass his power to kill,
Could prove it, to the hilt. More reason, then,
To make his best the fight in which he died.

V

But this he had not faced—that one would come
Well-schooled, well-armed, well-sinewed, but a knave,
A coward, screaming at the parried thrust,
Imploring mercy, a reverted slave
Grovelling to his master in the dust,
Fallen before the steel was driven home.

VI

Disgrace, disgust; the marrow in the bone
Turning to water. Had he not betrayed
The goddess, after all his victories,
By one so cheap, so foul, so base? His knees
Shook underneath him as he cleaned his blade
And vomited behind the altar-stone.

VII

Thereafter, he was never quite the same,
More bold, less wary, risking time and breath
In prayer, not search: would not the goddess purge

Her shrine, defiled, in chaste and awful wrath
Bid a defiant challenger emerge?
Part of his prayer was heard; no coward came.

VIII

No coward came, but those who came were still
Less than he prayed for. They were brave enough,
But lacked for something, strength or subtlety,
Feeble when wise, and ignorant when rough,
And always fewer than there used to be,
And easier than they ever were to kill.

IX

He might have, had he listened to the air,
Heard voices crying, "All the gods are gone,
Going, or gone." He might, far off, have heard
Rumor of rumor, echo of a word
Of temples down, barbarians coming on,
Failure of nerve, abandonment, despair.

X

He might have noticed that the pilgrim song
Rang out less heartily across the grove,
That in their times of silence they would stir
Uneasily, stir, and shift, and start, each move
The secret signal of a worshipper
Whose mind was elsewhere. There was something
        wrong.

XI

But nothing he could fathom. Wood and shore
Took all his diligence. His tenure held,
By now, more years than victims. One he felled
Proved, when he stripped the body for the flame,
A eunuch. After him, a woman came;
Long after her, a dwarf. And then no more.

XII

No stranger's footfall broke the trance. A bird
Sang, and was silent; wind and water made

Their customary murmur; there was no
Intruding presence, no alarm; the slow
Encroachment of the growing hosts of shade
Came slowly on; no human voice was heard . . .

XIII

. . . Hearken! a change, a different kind of noise
From the small creatures rustling in the brush,
Whispers, almost, or laughter choked, a queer
High-pitched excited interjection, "Hush!"—
The tongue is foreign, but the meaning clear.
The little animals are little boys.

XIV

Flat on their bellies, crawling low, they must
Use their wild fathers' artifice; they can
Be cats or serpents, wriggling closer toward
This old ridiculous long-bearded man
In the cracked armor, stabbing with his sword,
Stabbing, at what? ants running through the dust.

XV

And one breaks out of cover with a cry
More piercing than his wooden sword, bare chest
Scratched by the thorns, grimy with sweat and earth,
His charge his challenge. Watching him, the rest,
Standing, half split their sides with cruel mirth
To see their captain hack at hip and thigh.

XVI

An old man's prayer fulfilled! The ancient art
Runs down his shoulder through his wrist; the eyes,
Deep-sunk, burn bright with triumph, that the foe
Is here, is worthy; and he does not know
In his last moment, as he falls and dies,
His sword, once more, has pierced a warrior's heart.

SEER

The eyes are there, but so designed
All they can see is inward mind:
The veil is always drawn before
The luminous Lucretian shore;
These eyes do not behold the rain,
The sun, the cloud, the hill, the plain;
Not even phantoms of belief
Are doctor, lawyer, merchant, thief;
All the bright rush of evidence
Marshalled before the world of sense
Is nothing, less than nothing,—so
Phidippides, DiMaggio,
The Parthenon, the A & P,
Sharing invisibility,
Are equally conveyed, consigned
To the dominion of the blind.

And we, before this marble bust,
Reduced to particles of dust,
See, or suppose we see, the pure
Majestic God, serene and sure,
And in our fevered lives aspire
To his immortal lack of fire,
Immune and cool, beyond the strange
Phenomena of chance and change.

But these are not blind eyes. They burn
With passionate inward self-concern,
Most quick, most diligent, to mark
Each mode, each motion, in the dark,
Noting the Self's minutest move
With fond and fascinated love,
Forever fair, deluding us
Forever, wise, preposterous.

THE PRIVATE EYE

*(freely translated from the prose
of Raymond Chandler)*

There being, of public conscience, little or none,
We have, instead, The Private Eye, who sees
With keener insight than the common run,
Searches for hidden truths, solves mysteries,
And brings to book, or light, the fugitive,
The plot in which hunted and hunter live.

A liar when he has to be, a schemer
Deft in pursuit, a master of disguise,
He is our only one and true Redeemer,
No sacrificial lamb, but tough and wise,
A gambler and a follower of sport
Where sinners and/or publicans consort.

Down the mean streets he goes, himself not mean;
Down the dark streets he goes unterrified.
It is, indeed, no very fragrant scene
In which he earns a living; but his pride
Is like his honor, quick, instinctive, tense,
And he will suffer no man's insolence.

You must treat him as a proud man, or be sure
You will be very sorry. Cant and sham
Disgust him; he is relatively poor,
Does honest work, and does not give a damn
For protocol; is lonely, one of those
Who shock and frighten you with what he knows.

His talk is like his age's, witty, rude,
Hard-bitten; he can make his meaning clear,
Sometimes, in double-talk; his attitude
Toward women may be very cavalier,
It all depends. His sense of character
Exposes phony, jerk, and chiseller.

He is the hero, he is everything—
Common, complete, unusual, he must
Be better than the others, priest and king,
Defender of the Faith, In Whom We Trust.
Were there more like him, in that state of grace
Our world would be, withal, a safe, and brighter,
    place.

THE INNUMERABLE

"Sadness multiplies self."
                —Dr. Johnson

In the world of sorrow, where
Light is not, and all the host
Multiplies the single ghost
Dwelling on the lonely coast
In the solitary air,
Where the solid shade almost
Turns to substance, and the old
Boundaries of sense are lost,

Where no leaf is ever shaken
In the windless universe,
Where the vision dims and blurs
One to many wanderers,
Alternately found, forsaken,
Prisoners, imprisoners,
Loosing and renewing hold
In a land where nothing stirs,

There in all delight you move
Under myrtle's arching cover
Through the fields of mourning, over
Toward the far unmargined river,
Infinitely lost, in love,
Unaccompanied by lover
Save the self, made manifold,
Aisled and islanded forever.

RETURN

One maple, red already, says:
Prepare; be more than reconciled;
The Harvest Home at Summerfield
Will be a week from Thursday night.

The pictures of the football teams
Show, in the background, heavy shade;
The pear-tree, with its metal load,
On Gothic arch of iron bends.

Some apples fall; the Concords darken;
Niagaras, however, fill
Translucent-pale; along the wall
Berries of bitter-sweet begin.

The birds are few, but butterflies
Come black and double to the phlox;
Loose on its post, the letter-box
Holds nothing but one orange card,

Due notice of the town address.
Prepare; be more than reconciled.

HARVEST

This is a time of metal, not flesh or leaf:
The larches bronzen; the catalpas fade
Still green this side of gold, but yellowing;
White grapes, white gold; the grasshopper is jade;
Obsidian, the cricket creeps the stone.

And in the garden a brown lady, bending,
Takes dahlias or chrysanthemums, the sun
Turning the clippers copper as she moves,

No younger than she used to be, and harder
Than when I knew her once, in other days.

All this I see with no intense emotion,
With neither gross lament, nor undue praise,
Except that seeing is a form of praising,
And half the seasons out of all the years
Lament is natural to one beholding
The lady with the shears.

LULLABY

Night is dark and night is deep—
Sleep until the morning light.
All who lie awake alone
Reap in dust, along a site
Sown with thistles, rising tall,
Falling, to the scythe, on stone.

Stone dissolves, and towers fall;
Tall men in the dust are sown;
Sight grows dim, and widows reap
Lonely ground; no lamp at all
Lights the dusky chamber: sleep
Deep below the down of night.

RUNES FOR OLD BELIEVERS

(Counter-variation, on a theme by Cotton Mather)

The wolves of evening will be much abroad—
Hold to the twig of rowan—
When we are near the evening of the world.

The weather darkens: wilderness and wood
Thicken with stalkers; when the sun goes down
The wolves of evening will be much abroad.

Almost unseen, at dusk, across the field,
Gaunt-gray or shagbark-brown,
When we are near the evening of the world.

The herd their meat, their smell the smell of blood,
The ground their ground, the bolted house their own,
The wolves of evening will be much abroad.

The body, like the oak, is bent and gnarled,
The shallow-rooted mind is overthrown
When we are near the evening of the world.

If iron fails, and salt, and Aaron's rod,
Hold to the twig of rowan.
When we are near the evening of the world
The wolves of evening will be much abroad.

THE FOREST BACENIS

(Variation on themes from Julius Cæsar)

Here the barbarians never raid each other.
The forest intervenes
Of infinite magnitude,—thicket, tangle, vines
Reach from the nearer border to the farther.

And no man knows how far that border lies
Beyond his field, his home;
They have no way of measuring but time
To reckon boundaries.

Intrepid, traveling light, the lone explorer
Finds, right or left, the endless corridor,
The native wall, the dark eternal fortress
Against the threat of war.

So they are safe. They do not fear marauders,
The child enslaved, the virgin taken, grain
Burning at night, the cattle raids, the murders.
They call their lives their own.

Still, looking north or south, sometimes they wonder:
It might be good, they almost think, to dare
Beyond familiar limits, face adventure
More boldly, wander more.

That other land might prove
Richer than theirs, hospitable and friendly,
The girls exciting, they imagine fondly,
Expert at making love.

Or, if they were not welcome, they might enter
With an invading pride, be warriors
With something to remember in the winter
Around their warm and comfortable fires.

They lift their gaze, for one brief restless moment,
To where, below the shield, the swords hang crossed;
They breathe in deep, as if to blow the dust
Out of the plume of helmet.

But no. One thing they cannot face, the forest,
Dark, dark, through tangle, vine and thicket groping,
The smell of animals, the undergrowth,
The steaming moisture, rank with every horror.

They grow, at last, too tame for insurrection,
Inbred, content. They cross no boundary line.
They ask no more of any tribe or nation
Than to be left alone.

176

INDETERMINATE

Between the window and the night,
The maple stands beside my room,
Whose outward-going shaft of light
Pours like a river through the leaves,
Pours, and is broken by the leaves,
Whose motion makes a watery sound.
They rustle, and are still, resume
The restless ripple, stir, and slow
Wash of their move against the flow,
The stream, of light, which turns to sound
Somewhere, so interwoven, so
Shifting, so vague, no mind can mark
The borderline where light is sound
And sound diminishes to dark.

MARINE

Variation on a Theme by
Louise Townsend Nicholl

Waves that are white far out
Wear their way to the shore
Thunder running under.

The maned fall of the combers
Pours froth over, slowly,
Close in, and very shallow.

Waves that are white far out
Where the wind's will has its way
With water deep for sailing

Write long broken runes
In sand, for the poor student
To try construing over.

Waves that are white far out
Where treasure lies, deep down,
Fathoms below sounding,

Roll no richness here,
Only kelp to the margin,
Shell, or starfish, broken.

LOOKING UP AT AIRPLANES, ALWAYS

High overhead,
High overhead   the planes go over
I lift my eyes
To see them, always.

Having been there,
Having been there   at that great height
I rise up swiftly,
Am there again.

Like dragon-flies,
Like dragon-flies   how brief their season!
A hundred hours,
So I have heard.

PLAINS DRIVE

Space and sweep and speed
And silence—Oh, these are
Wonderfully good,
Riding in a car
Seventy miles an hour.

178

Over black and brown,
By grain, by gold, by green
Only rarely here,
Where the light and air
Lift the weary mood.

Even the great, the strong,
We have heard, go down
To the deep, dark water,
Black and very bitter.
Here no water lies,
No great mountains rise.

We must turn, we know,
Back where we belong,
To the little town
At the mountain's base,
Facing peak and cloud.

Turn southwestward, face
Slant of storm, and loud
Rushing mighty wind,
Only, as we go,
Keeping in the mind
Sweep and speed and space,
Light and quietude

THE SEASONS

"All the seasons are riders."
—Norbert Fagan

They all are riders: Spring on a two-year-old,
A chestnut colt, with a green way of going,
Azure and saffron halves, with pink cross sashes,
And a whip with blossoms on it, forsythia-gold.

Summer, all green, blue cap, on a distance runner
In a good field, dark bay or black or brown,
Getting the distance handily, well-lathered,
Yet coming back ears forward, far from blown.

Autumn in scarlet coat, a tanned outrider
On a fat piebald pony, whom they all
Troop after in parade, in bright decorum,
Toward the last race in the fall.

And Winter a hollow-cheeked, gaunt, grizzled jockey,
Forcing an old gray jumper, whose white breath
Steams on the air, over the black rail fences,
Across the snow, in at the fox's death.

THE GREEN-SICK GIRLS

*"The spiritual malady of our time
is a sort of green sickness in girls."*
—Charles G. Bell

The green-sick girls loll under the willow-trees
With spines as limp as so many lime Jell-os;
They have an excuse from home-work and athletics,
And they never romp with the fellows.

The green-sick girls are clad in chartreuse frocks;
Their complexions are too chlorotic to be good-look-
ing,
And the only time they show any emotion at all
Is when they feel like puking.

Oh, the green-sick girls, the green-sick girls are a bore,
For whom we possibly ought to feel more compassion
Were it not for the fact that most of us, most of the
time,
Go around in just that fashion.

180

BALLADE OF
THE LISTLESS COURT LADIES

There are no wonders any more;
Marvels are gone from earth and air.
The waves break gray along a shore
Under a cloud of gray despair
No banners fly, no bugles blare,
No silver string, no golden horn
Makes lovely music anywhere.
We've never seen a unicorn.

No key unlocks the magic door,
No prince ascends the magic stair.
There are no wonders any more.
No princess, with her loosened hair,
Comes to her knight's embrace; we share
The wish that we were never born.
The wells are dry, the woods are bare;
We've never seen a unicorn.

There are no wonders any more.
Energy equals MC square,
And two and two are always four,
And who are we to think we care?
All the enchantments, old and rare,
Are runes we cannot read; forlorn
Under persimmon-tree, or pear,
We've never seen a unicorn.

L'Envoi

My lord, beware, my lord, beware
The folly of belief outworn!
By all our lassitude, we swear
We've never seen a unicorn.

BALLADE OF KILROY

Now is the world in a terrible way
Under the gathering clouds of gloom:
Love is a witless emigré
Vainly hunting a furnished room;
The crash will surely follow the boom,
Mourners will trail behind the bier.
What can be done about this? by whom?
Look! it is written—*Kilroy was here,*

What has become of the Celtic Yea,
The affirmation of Molly Bloom?
Who is intrepid enough to say,
"Dr. Livingstone, I presume"?
Everyone delves in the depths of the tomb,
And only rubble and shards appear;
Everyone wants to go back to the womb:
Look! it is written—*Kilroy was here.*

Where are the bonny, the blithe, the gay?
Gone with the wind, or down the flume
With the snows and roses of yesterday.
The bride's unable to come to the groom.
Statesmen bicker and piddle and fume
While Death rides high in the stratosphere.
What we need is a brand-new broom:
Look! it is written—*Kilroy was here.*

L'Envoi

Prince, when the peal of the crack of doom
Breaks on the apprehensive ear,
Buckle the armor; up with the plume—
Look! it is written—*Kilroy was here.*

THE NOVEMBER SHINE

Not now the oil-black shimmer of summer on the
    road,
But a gray glare, still glare, though, and still bright
Enough to narrow eyes against. We smell
The smoke, again, of burning leaves—how trite
A thing to say, or notice!—and the car
Swings to the left-hand lane, and on our right
We pass a truck, two kids in the back, and one
A tow-head, with a casque of shining white.
The road-side stands have rows of pumpkins, late,
Too late for Hallowe'en, too small for suns,
But huge for pumpkins, seamed and orange, burning
Beside the smoother cider-jars, whose light
Flashes an amber dazzle, lamps in day-time.
With the leaves gone, or almost, sunlight blinds,
Reflected from smooth bark or bough, and sky
Is quiet gray-blue lake, or bay, as far as eye
Can see, or tell. Less color, to be sure,
Less warmth, no heavy shade, less green, but still
Not yet enough of sharpness nor of chill
To shiver for, or wind the windows tight.
So far, November's need supplies its answer—
More light, more light.

GREEN ARMOR ON
GREEN GROUND

Y mae'r llyfr hwn i Dyddgu—
fy nyolch a fy ngharu.

Introduction

What we know of the Welsh seems mighty little, compared
with what we think we know of the Scotch or Irish. An invid-
ious nursery rhyme; some lampoonery, not without rough
admiration, in Shakespeare: what else? A contumacious people,
they seem to have been, the Cymri, confederates never any
longer than they had to be, fighting with, and beaten by, Romans, Saxons, Normans, Danes, Irish, turning around, as often
as not, and mauling their oppressors, coming home victorious,
to betray their leaders and fall to feuding, repeating the cycle.
Yet, at their best, a people seemly and brave; you could never,
says Powys, really bribe them or really scare them. They possessed, he adds, an intense delight in little things; and no less
an authority than the Keeper of Manuscripts in the British
Museum refers to them as "buoyant, gay, and sensuous, fond
of bright colors and eager for life." That, to be sure, may have
been before coal mines and Calvinism, but to this day, we
know, they are great honorers of music and song.

Of their literary tradition we are also considerably in the
dark. Taliesin, one of their bards, gave, we have heard, the
architect Frank Lloyd Wright the name of one of his houses.
Our scholars know of Giraldus Cambrensis and claim Geoffrey
of Monmouth for the Cymri; tales from the White Book and
the Red, from Rhydderch and Hergest, have been given us in

Lady Guest's translations from the Mabinogion. *Ar hyd y nos,* and *Rhyfegyrch Gwyr Harlech,* we may have heard sung, by tenor or chorus, live or on recordings. The word Eisteddfod we know, and can mispronounce with the next man. And that's about all.

Dylan Thomas, in a posthumous article which appeared in *The Atlantic Monthly,* stated his belief that the old bardic meters were too difficult to be adapted successfully into the English tongue. If true, it would be a great pity, for the effects of which those old meters are capable, even if only partially followed, suggest much that might enrich the texture of our verse patterns. Using, for their basic unit, not the beat, but a syllable count, the Welsh permit, even insist on, all sorts of subtle shifts in the cadences, the rhythms, of the line; they produce, so, a much more effective kind of counterpoint than is the norm in English. Their use of off-rhyme is possibly less novel to us, this last century, since we know the practice, fairly familiarly, in the work of Emily Dickinson, Wilfred Owen, Auden and others. And one more thing they do, by which we might stand to profit; they love to rhyme, not merely down the righthand column, but from right to center as well, weaving the rhyme words into the entire texture, not just an end-word, lop-sided sort of business. And then there is the whole matter of *Cynghanedd,* the harmony, the interlocking, by alliteration, assonance, and rhyme, all through the lines. That really is hard, but how beautiful, the way they bring it off!

I santesau	oes un tasel
a wna teiau	onid Hywel,
o fewn caerau	o fain cwrel
i bawb copiau	o bob capel;
Un â llengau	yn null angel
o nef enwau	yn ei fanwel
a rydd sensau,	urddas honsel
elusennau	oel a sinnel.

For my own discovery of the Twenty-four Official Meters, as well as for much other information and delight, I am indebted to the book *An Introduction to Welsh Poetry* (From the Beginnings to the Sixteenth Century), by Gwyn Williams, published by Faber & Faber, in London, in 1953. In my appendix I have presented, somewhat sketchily following Mr. Williams, the technical requirements of these measures; and have also added, in brief, some indication of the various types of *Cynghanedd,* to which, in the poems themselves, I am afraid I have paid only token observance. But there is enough here, I hope, to encourage somebody else to go ahead and do better. *Blodeued Cymru!*

ROLFE HUMPHRIES

New York City
June, 1955

FOR MY ANCESTORS

(Cyhydedd fer)

Wales, which I have never seen,
Is gloomy, mountainous, and green,
And, as I judge from reading Borrow,
The people there rejoice in sorrow,
Dissenters, most of them, and cranks,
Surly and churlish, grudging thanks,
Suspicious, dour, morose, perplexed,
And just a little oversexed.
Mostly, however, they go in
More for remorsefulness than sin,
The latter being prior to
The real delight, of feeling blue.
Fellows named Morgan, Evans, Jones,
Sit glumly on the ancient stones,
And men with names in—IES,
Like mine, lurk in the wilderness
With conscience riding on their shoulders
Heavier than the native boulders.
The weather veers from dim to foul,
The letter W's a vowel;
They dig in mines, they care for sheep,
Some kinds of promises they keep;
They can remember warriors found
Dead in green armor on green ground;
They practice magic out of season,
They hate the English with good reason,
Nor do they trust the Irish more,
And find the Scots an utter bore.

However grim their life, and hard,
One thing they dearly love, a bard.
Even the meanest hand at lays
Is plied with ale, and crowned with bays,
And set with honor in their books
Above even liars, thieves, and crooks.
This is the one redeeming grace
That saves them for the human race,
This is their claim to virtue; therefore,
Though there is much I do not care for
In my inheritance, I own
This impulse in my blood and bone,
And so I bend a reverent knee,
O Cymric ancestor, to thee,—
Wild Wales forever! Foul or fair,
This tribute from a grateful heir.

IN PRAISE OF TENBY

(Englyn Penfyr)

High over the sea stands a fine stronghold,
Old, but less old than the long
Beat and boom of ocean song

At its base, where each ninth comber breaks loud
With proud outcry, flinging foam
At the great gray cliff, the home

Of sea-mew, osprey, ern. And there, up high,
Sky-near, walled well, is a fair
Fine gathering, with good share

Of meat for all, and Oh, plenty of mead
Indeed, for bards from the glen,
For harpers and singing men.

They have climbed wet stair, dark shale, in pride and
    glory,
From the low drone of the tide
To the promontory's wide

Mansions of music, where singing wood and voice,
Rejoicing in brotherhood,
Sound their great glee, the full flood

Poured to the sky, above the soaring bird,
Or heard below on the shore
With ocean's old rush and roar

Subdued, the mournful measures fading under
The thunder of this cascade,
This jubilation's cadence.

AROUND THANKSGIVING

(Englyn Milwr)

Pure gold, they said in her praise:
So I walk my autumn ways,
Around me a golden haze

From the ground, in leaves, in air—
Oh, everywhere, everywhere!—
To save, to spend, and to share.

By the door, with evening light,
Westering, lingering late
Over lane and lawn and lot

The leaves of the lilac hold
The shape of the heart, *pure gold,*
As if I need to be told,

As if I need reminding,
Toward chill November's ending,
Of warmth and love abounding.

SHAFT AND WINGS OF
THE WAY IT WAS ONCE

(Englyn unodl union)

Luerius, King of the Arverni,
Riding, near or far,
Had huntsmen, hounds, and harpers
Round his silver-mounted car.

In his high hall, at the head table, there
Was where his high bard fed.
The king's son gave him bread
And a princess poured his mead.

Twenty-four gold crowns he was always given
When a girl wed in the hall.
All raids conveyed him spoil,
A red bull or a black bull.

Stallion or falcon, greyhound, swan, or bow,
Or a book to look upon,
Or a bright jewel-stone,
For the asking, were his own.

Around him younger men, in green linens,
With golden torques, were seen
Learning to link the tune
Quietly for the queen.

No churl's son could learn these three professions:
Futile for one to be
Scholar or smith, or essay
The arts of poetry.

They trained, the bards, and drank with fighters, rode
On raids by day or by night.
They tripled what they taught.
They fought as well as they wrote.

Tough and gay, they had the gift and the knack,
The know of it all, the craft,
The light in the heart, the lift
Of music when they laughed.

The wildness of the sea they were in fight,
Fine nets for the love of girls.
So it was once in the world.
What are we,—sons of churls?

FOR A WORDFARER

(Englyn Unodl Crwca)

Speak them slowly, space them so:
Say them soft, or sing them low,
Words whose way we may not know any more.
Still, before the days go,

Sing them low, or say them soft.
Such a little while is left
To counterpoint the soundless drift of Time,
Let rhyming fall and lift.

Space them so, with lift and fall
Decent in their interval,
Late, archaic, who could say?—but always
Graceful, musical.

194

THE LAMENT
OF LLYWARCH HEN

(Englyn Cyrch)

Wooden staff, the time has come
Of the fall of leaf, autumn.
Bracken reddens; all those men
Who praised Llywarch Hen are dumb.

Ere my back was bent, I led
Men in war; that is ended.
Straight and tough, my spear was good,
Sure to draw first blood, bright red.

Wooden staff, now I have no
Smooth white arm for my pillow.
Not one slender one, or sly,
Waits to watch where I might go.

Ere my back was bent, I had
More than one canty comrade.
All the lusty men of Wales
Drew me free what ales they had.

Wooden staff, my bed is hard;
Stubble pales; birds fly southward.
No one visits me, no girl;
No man hails me, churl or bard.

Ere my back was bent, I once
Took delight in bay stallions,
Raced and rode with Llawr and Gwen,
Two upstanding men, my sons.

Wooden staff, when Llawr and Gwen
Fell in fight, I was broken.
Field is barren, fire is cold
For all sonless older men.

Coughing, misery, old age
Rack me now, do me damage.
Carrion am I, no less,
In my wilderness or cage.

From the hour he left the womb
Llywarch carried one heirloom,
Grief and labor, a great load
Down his lonely road of doom.

MERIONETH

(Englyn proest dalgron)

In that sweet, mild western air
Castle stones are russet fire,
Wind goes gentle, water clear,
A minute is a quarter hour.

Golden broom on mountainside,
Golden gorse along the road,
Rowan, oak, and alder shade
Lower ground with globe of cloud.

While their afternoon wears on,
Old men, sitting in the sun,
Warm on ankle bone and shin,
Do not envy any man.

Slanting over shire and shore,
Cader Idris, Traeth Mawr,
Light is rich, though folk be poor,
In that sweet, mild western air.

BENISON

(Englyn lleddfbroest)

Though her breathing seem a sigh
Never break her slumber's joy.
Sleep is caring for her now;
Sleep will do as much for you.

Be the weather fair or foul,
Sleep together, sleep a while.
Angels at the vestibule
Wait with honey, wine and oil,

For the wakeners to use
In fulfillment of their vows
On their pilgrimage to joys
Pleasanter than Paradise.

Gently, lovers, turn and join,
So commingle, so commune,
While the good Saint Valentine
Sends his holy blessing down.

A CHAIN-CHARM FOR A LADY

(Englyn Proest Gadwynog)

Water-bulrush, water-willow
From the margin of the hollow
Shade thy bed and shape thy pillow,
Time be slow and apple-mellow.

If the sun to cloud hath gone
Take the shadow for thy gain;
Wait thy moment; soon the lawn
Glows and goldens, very soon.

197

In the wind at evening, hear
More than air gather, pour
Water-music for the ear
Of the fonder listener.

Count from one to seven, slowly;
Look up bold, or look down shyly;
Dream of asphodel and moly
Growing in an ancient valley.

Cadence break, or cadence bind
High in air or under ground,
Past the measure of the mind,
Out of reach of any hand.

HARP MUSIC

*(The alternate stanzas,
respectively, Awdl gywydd,
and Cywydd deuair hirion)*

Softly, let the measure break
Till the dancers wake, and rise,
Lace their golden shoes, and turn
Toward the stars that burn their eyes.

Softly, let the measure flow,
Float in silver, and follow.

Softly, let the measure dwell
Slowly, as the spell is wound
Out and in, through space and time,
While the sandals rhyme the round.

Softly, let the measure stir,
Lift, subside, and go under.

Softly, let the measure prove
The bright cadence moving there
Changing, for unbroken dark,
The illumined arc of air.

Softly, let the measure be
Unheard, but never wholly.

CYMRIC LOVE SONG

(Cywydd deuair hirion)

On the side of a hill
In the month of April

I was with her
In wonderful weather.

Do you ask me to tell
Of myth or of marvel?

No one said *No!*
From height or from hollow.

In what other country
Would I rather be?

Or whose way of moving
Should I more sing?

I will dwell on her praise
For now and for always.

FROM THE
GREEN BOOK OF YFAN *

(Cywydd deuair fyrion)

Margaret Morse,
Mistress of horse,
Marshalled a troop
Matched, head to croup,
Marched through the dales
Mauling all males.

Normandy's knights,
Noting such sights,
Never drew rein
Not till they came
North to the firth
Now called the Forth.

Ocean and oar
Opened no door.
Over the weirs
Omens and fears,
Odors of mould.
Only the old

Pity the proud.
Purple through cloud,
Peregrines knive,
Plummet and dive.

* The Green Book of Yfan, the proper name being either an archaic form of Evan or a truncated version of Myfanwy (scholars are uncertain), is a manuscript of highly dubious provenance and authenticity. Its few tattered and defaced pages contain little of poetic worth. The fragment above was presumably part of a longer alphabetical chronicle like the medieval *Battle of Fontenoy*. It seems possible that through a scribe's error two entirely different poems have been here confused, for the tone of the O, P, and possibly R, stanzas seems markedly unlike the rest.

200

Pards on the prowl
Pybass * the owl.

Quentin the Queer,
Quaffing his beer,
Quoted a million
Quips from Quintilian.
Quince-tree and pear
Quavered in air.

Rolfe, for renown,
Wrote this all down,
Runes on a page
Rotting with age,
Ruined by Time,
Ruthless to rhyme.

* In verbs of this highly spondaic quality it is permissible
license, for metrical effect, or by special dispensation from the
Penkerdd, or Chief Poet, to transpose initial consonants, pro-
viding they are mute plosives, or plosive mutes.

CYCLE

(Cywydd deuair fyrion)

Bells in autumn
Toll a rhythm
Slow and solemn
Calling welcome
To the kingdom
Of the lonesome.

Can a sound throw
Any shadow?
The sift of snow
Fills the furrow.
Whose white arrow
Fells the hero?

No trace of her,
Morning's daughter,
Here or yonder.
The pale watcher
By green water
Knows the answer.

The bells of spring
Will be ringing,
Branches blossom,
And she will come
Out of darkness,
All bright, to bless,
Heal and hallow,
And, as we know,
Evoke new stir,
Growth and wonder.

THE CHAMPION

(Cywydd llosgyrnog)

Beyond the outskirts of the town
The buses park, the folk step down.
Who wins the crown of the bard?
Now every inch of Rhyll's green sod
Is taken for the Eisteddfod:
The test, by God, will be hard.

The match is on; no football game,
No tennis tournament,—the aim
For which they came being song.
The music, rising wave on wave,
Gives, more than combat ever gave,
Proof of the brave and the strong.

Robed in their blue or white or green,
Solemn and bearded, tall and lean,
Of Druid mien, the old men,
One in a golden corselet, go,
Better to listen, to and fro,
Over and over again.

Late in the day, they summon one
To honor's place, the golden throne,
There to be known as the best.
Hebog, the Hawk, puts on the crown
As the six-foot sword is drawn, sheathed, drawn,
And the sun goes down in the west.

WINTER, OLD STYLE

(Rhupunt)

Keen is the wind,
Barren the land.
A man could stand
On a single stalk.

Cattle are lean,
The stag is thin,
All color wan
On the frozen lake.

Idle the shield
On an old man's shoulder.
Halls are cold.
I have a wound.

Where warriors go
I cannot follow
Through flying snow
In this wild wind.

The trees are bowed
In the bare wood;
There is no shade
In any vale.

The reeds are dry
And a loud crying
Howls outside
The horse's stall.

The light is short.
Sorrow and hurt
Harry the heart
With inward war.

So an old man
Does what he can,
Stares through the pane
At night's black square.

THE LABYRINTH

(Byr a thoddaid)

Dark is this maze wherein I err.
No Theseus I; no comforter,
No Ariadne at my side, to hold
Her golden skein as guide.

Dark is this maze; I cannot see
The sword held out in front of me.
I have no shield; my other arm must find
The blind way through this harm.

Dark is this maze, roofed in, with vault and stair
Where I must often halt,
Descend or climb, wait, listen, hear
The skipping heartbeat of my fear.

Dark is this maze, but I must know it more,
Explore, before I go
Free to the light, the pit, the den,
Whose two-formed monster feeds on men.

I hear him bellow, far from here.
I feel, I smell him, very near.
I spin, I strike a blow that finds no mark.
Dark is this maze. I know.

THE LORE OF PRYDERI

(Clogyrnach)

Follow the feather down the air,
Save fernseed from the maidenhair,
Study on the tide
Straws that drift and slide
Down the wide ocean stair

Or to the darker forest go,
Step quietly, but sure, but slow,
Find on rock the pale
Silver track of snail,
Seek the frail print of doe.

Pryderi learned this, taught this, knew
Much more than Powyl meant him to,
Marvels on the most
Solitary coast,
Host on host, fire in dew,

Brightness in dark, and bread in stone,
So, bred of Sorrow's flesh and bone,
Wisdom, grown, retains
All his father's gains,
Adds domains all his own.

205

Oh, mist and moss and feather and fern,
As all King Wisdom's minstrels learn,
In the darkest days,
Flash their motes of praise,
Glow and blaze, shine and burn.

WMFFRE THE SWEEP

(Cyhydedd Naw Ban)

Wmffre the Sweep was mad as a mink,
Covered with cinders, blacker than ink,
Didn't mind darkness, didn't mind stink;
Light was his loathing, light made him blink
Coming through crevice, cranny or chink.
Drank through his whiskers, dust in his drink.

Wretched the ways of Wmffre the Sweep:
Little to gain, and nothing to keep;
Labor was plenty, labor was cheap,
Filthy the flues, and chimneys were steep;
Grimy, red-eyed, unable to weep,
Home to his pallet, ugly in sleep.

Wmffre the Sweep beheld a strange sight
In his day's dark or in the real night:
Ninety-nine angels, harnessed in light,
Michael among them, bearded and bright,
Majesty moving, melody, might—
Wmffre the Sweep was inspired to write.

Wmffre the Sweep, a lout and a clod,
Fed all his life on cabbage and cod,
Housed in a hovel, never well-shod,
Shouldering buckets, besoms and hod,
Shovelled, like all men, under the sod,
Left a great poem, praise of his God.

DAFYDD AP GWILYM HATES
DYDDGU'S HUSBAND

(Cyhydedd Hir)

'Tis sorrow and pain,
'Tis endless chagrin
For Dafydd to gain
His dark-haired girl.
Her house is a gaol,
Her turnkey a vile
Sour, yellow-eyed, pale
Odious churl.

She cannot go out
Unless he's about,
The blackguard, the lout,
The stingy boor.
The look in her eye
Of fondness for me—
God bless her bounty!—
He can't endure.

I know he hates play:
The greenwood in May,
The birds' roundelay,
Are not for him.
The cuckoo, I know,
He'd never allow
To sing on his bough,
Light on his limb.

The flash of the wing,
The swell of the song,
Harp-music playing,
Draw his black looks.
The hounds in full cry,
A race-horse of bay,
He cannot enjoy
More than the pox.

207

My heart would be glad
At seeing him laid
All gray in his shroud;
How could I grieve?
Should he die this year,
I'd give him, with cheer,
Good oak for his bier,
Sods for his grave.

O starling, O swift,
Go soaring aloft,
Come down to the croft
By Dyddgu's home.
This message give her,
Tell her I love her,
And I will have her,
All in good time.

THE TYLWYTH TEG

(Toddaid)

The Tylwyth Teg live in caves and mountains;
Far under the waves they fold their herds.
As beautiful as the day, their women
Are wise in the way of beasts and birds.

If won as wives by the folk in valleys,
They will bring good luck; they understand
Simples and herbs, and in harvest season
Helpers come far at their command.

The Tylwyth Teg are not above stealing
The corn they love, or churns, or rings,
Or feathers, or veils, or leather harness—
Light-fingered they are at taking things.

On a market-day they may come to town.
It's a rule of thumb that trade is good
Whenever they do, but one thing for sure,
And no use being misunderstood,

They will talk in signs, they will say no word,
And one thing more, pay the closest heed
Never to let them be touched with iron,
From iron they flee with panic speed.

There are bad ones among the Tylwyth Teg:
They will leave their children in your cot
When their brats be ugly, and take your own
Before you can wake, as like as not.

From Llyn y Fan Fach, from Carmarthenshire,
From near and from far, from Llyn Du'r Addu,
From Llyn y Forwyn, from Aberglaslyri,
These stories we hear; they must be true.

LLANELLY COTTAGE

(Gwawdodyn)

A light-capped sea, and a bird-bright shore—
Whatever else was I looking for,
With sun at my back, blue sky above me?
A dark-haired girl by an open door.

A dark-haired girl in a scarlet dress,
An invitation from loveliness:
Will you touch me deep, will you share my sleep,
Will you come, or keep me comfortless?

The sun at my back, blue sky above,
But over that sill who would not move?
For the light-capped sea and the bird-bright shore
Said never a word against my love.

The scarlet dress came over her head,
Her skin was as white as her silken bed:
*Whisper me softly, pleasure me deftly,
Leave me not swiftly,* she said, she said.

The sea, light-capped, and the shore, bird-bright,
By day outdoors are a shining sight,
But a scarlet dress, over chair or floor,
Silk bed, and dark hair, are fine for night.

THE RUNES
OF ARHOLFAN CYMRO

(Gwawdodyn Hir)

Cloud over hill, cloud over hollow:
Why do you wait beside your window?
The south wind sighs, a sound of sorrow.
From far away the faint horns echo.
The hours are long, the daylight slow to leave.
For the moment, grieve in the shadow.

Darkness may be the time. The quarrel
Wants resolution. Light the candle,
Be gowned in red and gold apparel,
Murmur, *Deliver us from evil,*
And cross the sill, descend the marble stair,
Pause there and pose there, not too mournful.

Hear, over the music or under,
The wonderful wish of the water,
Reunion of lover and lover
In the light, the ardor of summer,
Not very high and not very far,
And all a green arbor and bower.

Cloud on the moor, cloud on the mountain:
The apples fall; the torches darken;
The guards resume their ancient station.
Lord God, why did you make the craven?
There was a time when wounded men were
        proud,—
Cloud over dune, cloud over ocean.

THE SONS OF ST. DAVID

(Hir a Thoddaid)

*—Lie still, ye thief, and hear the lady
sing in Welsh.* The first part of KING
HENRY IV, Act III, Scene I.

Lie still, ye thief, and hear the lady sing
In her own language, the confederates' tongue
Old Llywarch used, and Heledd, for their longing—
Blossom on branch, and osprey on the wing,
And Olwen's footprint in the morning mist.
Lie still, ye thief; listen to the song.

Lie still, lie still; and hear harp-music, far
Beyond Time's arras, feud, betrayal, war,
Bereavement and self-pity—all they are,
And all they were, they faced. They said, *Yea, sure!*
Look you, they said; they looked both near and high.
Lie still, ye rogue, lie still; hear the air.

Lie still, and listen, for the Cymri know
Measures of mirth and melodies of sorrow,
The dragon's track, drawn red across the snow,
White hawthorn, golden pear, the darker shadow
A girl's hair makes above the pillow's mound.
Hearken to the sound, and its echo.

211

Lie still, ye silly flouter of Glendower.
A fair young queen sings in her summer bower,
An old man in the winter of his power
Fingers the harp-strings, and the golden shower,
The golden rain, descends to light our dark.
Lie still, Hotspur; hearken for an hour.

ABERDOVEY MUSIC

(Cyrch a chwta)

The bells of Aberdovey
Sound from a buried city
Sunken far under the sea,
Heard when the nights are stormy
And carried inland, faintly,
As far as Montgomery.
Hearken! Music of the lost
Haunts that coast, all shadowy.

And there could be voices there,
Leagues and fathoms down, a choir
Whose intoning reaches far
Out along that lonely shore
Up to ghostly cloud and air,
Cadences profound and pure,
Solemn choral, when the bell
Has tolled the knell of the hour.

As winds on earth go over,
Aeolian-wise, to stir
Response of harp or zither,
So, under ocean-water,
Currents deeper and stronger
Sweep strings of salt and silver
In their ultramarine room,
Break off, resume, and linger.

Hearken again! Is the lull
Pause of canticle or bell,
Rest or silence? Who can tell?
During this calm interval
The stones of sarn and sea-wall
Come closer; call to them, call
The music, sound or echo,
From undertow and ground-swell.

OAK

(Tawddgyrch cadwynog)

It is lonely.
In these short days
Without her praise
I, too, grow less.

The Druids' tree
Is far more wise
In the mean ways
Of wintriness,

Clings to the leaf,
However dry,
Will not deny
By letting go.

Seasons are brief,
Sorrow goes by;
Hold on till May,
This will be over.

This will be gone,
Hill, field, and stream
Ripple and gleam
In supple gloss

Of shining sun,
And waking seem
A healing dream,—
Oh yes, oh yes!

THE DRUIDS

In the evenings, in the clearings, in the forest
That is where they often would be found,
Tall under the low dull solemn oaks, but shorter
Than their shadows falling on the ground.

Exempt from war, if they went down in battle,
They would refuse all aid;
They were versed in many mysteries, and music
Was what they always made;

And in time of peace, they were very good with the oar,
And soft with women, silent in any grief;
And they also knew the use of the beater's maul
On the pliant golden leaf.

VARIATION ON A THEME
FROM FRANCIS KILVERT

The Welch harp has no silver string,
And it is played on the left shoulder.
And the harpers all are older
Than the counsellors of the king.

And they are becoming rare,
Those gray and bearded men
With young hands and long fingers,

But every here and there,
By glade or coombe or glen,
One of them lingers

Remote from all known ways
Save those that music clears
Through ash and sycamore
To the door of their dwelling.

Whenever one of them plays,
Whoever hears him hears
Most beautiful old airs.

They are poor of purse; they rise
May mornings, very early,
And tradesmen think they are surly
In spite of the wrinkled eyes
Scored by years of smiling.

AIR, FROM THE OLD WELSH

Like seaweed under water,
The uneventful trees
Move at my window
In the mist of the morning.

If I could count the leaves
And multiply them by
The number of seasons left me,
And were every leaf a love,
There would still not be enough
To have before I die.

Ah, what stubborn stuff
I waken to find
In the cells of the mind
On the sills of the morning.

"A GREEN PRIDE"

A green pride of green leaves
Was all about that summer place,
While the hour of the sheaves
Waited, over the hill

Whose pretence of being far,
Far in time, far in space,
Lulled and held summer still.
Still, the flower was the flower,

Not one petal falling.
Motion left to the air,
To the paper-thin veer
Of the butterfly's going.

A green pride of green leaves
Over arbor, lawn, bower,
And the hour of the sheaves,
Even so, coming closer.

SONG FROM THE GAELIC, MAYBE

The fond summer numbers
Fade from eye and ear;
The angler in the stream
Is no more there.
For all one remembers
The sigh comes easy,
The long-drawn sigh
For the green wish of summer
Going by, gone by—
Dream and illusion,
Illusion and dream,
And the fisherman gone
Like the fly from the stream.

In the streets of the town
People appear
Dressed for the season
In jackets and sweaters.
So many good creatures!
And some of them, cheery
Out of all reason—
(Oh, not you! And not I!)—
Stoutly maintain,
Avow and aver
And insist on declaring
The white wall of winter
Is also a lie.

DAFYDD AP GWILYM
RESENTS THE WINTER

Across North Wales
The snowflakes wander,
A swarm of white bees.
Over the woods
A cold veil lies.
A load of chalk
Bows down the trees.

No undergrowth
Without its wool,
No field unsheeted;
No path is left
Through any field;
On every stump
White flour is milled.

Will someone tell me
What angels lift
Planks in the flour-loft
Floor of heaven,

Shaking down dust?
An angel's cloak
Is cold quicksilver.

And here below
The big drifts blow,
Blow and billow
Across the heather
Like swollen bellies.
The frozen foam
Falls in fleeces.

Out of my house
I will not stir
For any girl
To have my coat
Look like a miller's
Or stuck with feathers
Of eider down.

What a great fall
Lies on my country!
A wide wall, stretching
One sea to the other,
Greater and grayer
Than the sea's graveyard.
When will rain come?

NIGHT SONG

OF DAFYDD AP GWILYM

All this I was doing
Over a girl,
In loneliness going
Across the bare moor
And through the blind night
In the pitch of the darkness,
Lost from the high road.

Through many ridged fields,
Down slopes that were soggy,
Over stubble and furrow
With stumble and sorrow,
Through nine thorny thickets,
By ruined old forts,
To the brow of the mountain,

And missing the bogs
And their green habitation
Whose hateful companions
Circled around me,
A fighter betrayed
In the thick of the battle,
A man in a gaol.

But worse than the fogs
And all desolation
Were the spirits of evil
Circling around me,
And my crossing and praying,
My charming and rhyme
Of little avail.

This took a long time:
But at last I looked up
And there were the stars!
Like cherries they were
In the orchards of night,
All yellow and red,
All shining and bright.

The sparks of the bonfires
Of seven dear saints,
The gems of the host
In the harness of heaven,
The pickets of embers
Whose orbits are long
And wind cannot take them.

I stopped in my tracks,
And "Look you," I said,
"This is over and done.
She will have to be told,
God forgive me the telling,
I'll travel no more
To the door of her dwelling
Through any such going
Nor blunt my good axe
On the face of the stone."

A BRECON VERSION

Whoever Trystan drew blood on,
That man surely fell.
Whoever drew blood on Trystan,
That man also fell.
King March sent to King Arthur
How to loose that spell.

Trystan took Queen Essylt
To Celyddon's green wood.
Trystan took Queen Essylt
In Celyddon's green wood.
King March rode to King Arthur,
Burning as he rode.

King Arthur gave him counsel:
"The only thing to do,
The only thing for you
Is send him many harpers
To play him from afar,
And poets to praise him near."

King March sent poets and harpers
Who did as they were told,
And Trystan gave them silver,

And Trystan gave them gold.
Then they brought Gwalchmai to him
In a corselet all of gold,

Gwalchmai, son of Gwyar,
Chief peacemaker of them all.
Gwalchmai, son of Gwyar,
Took Trystan to Arthur's hall.
Arthur made peace between them,
Trystan and King March.

He spoke with both together,
He spoke with each apart.
Trystan said he wanted
Queen Essylt with all his heart.
King March said he wanted
Queen Essylt with all his heart.

King Arthur said one should have her
While the leaves were on the trees,
And the other one should have her
While the leaves were off the trees.
He gave King March the choosing,
Since he her husband was.

King March said he would have her
When the leaves were off the trees.
He said the nights were longer
When the leaves were off the trees.
King March bethought him clever
Leaving summer to her lover.

When Arthur told Queen Essylt,
She said, "O blessèd be
The judgment and its giver!"
She made her courtesy
And rose up from her knee,
And danced and sang to the measure:

"There are three trees that are good,
Holly, yew, and ivy-wood.
There are three trees that keep
Their leaves forever and always,
And always and forever
With Trystan I will sleep."

RHIANNON'S AIR

I go my errand
In my own manner:
By land or water
In my own way
I go my quest
    And the light falls, lightly.

And all my warblers
Make such sweet music
No man who hears
Can be a warrior
For eighty years
    And the light falls, lightly.

Across the meadows,
Through woodland shadows,
By night or day
In my own way
I go my errand
    And the light falls, lightly.

So follow me slowly,
O my dear pursuer,
Only remember
In my own way
I go my quest
    And the light falls, lightly.

THE CYNNEDDF

After a banquet
Powyll of Dyfed
With many attending
Strolled to a hillock
Back of the palace.

"Lord," said a courtier,
"Here is a strangeness:
If you sit on this mound
One of two things
Will certainly happen
Before you depart,—
The hurt of a wound
Or the sight of a wonder."

"I fear no wound,"
Said Powyll of Dyfed
"With this host all around me,
And as for a wonder,
Gladly I'd see one,
For wonders were ever
Dear to my heart."

He sat on the mound,
And a lady came riding,
Lovely to look at
In garments of gold
On a cream-colored stallion.
She rode very slowly,
She sang sweet and low,
And no one there knew her.

Powyll of Dyfed
Followed on foot
And could not overtake her,
And sent for the sorrel,
Most fleet of his stable,

Mounted and rode
By cairn and by cromlech.

Salmon and eagle,
The owl and the ousel,
From rock and from river,
From water, from air,
Watched the pursuit,
Pursued and pursuer.

Weary of riding,
Powyll of Dyfed
Cried in despair
To the beautiful lady
"Stay, in the name
Of the one you love best!"

She reined in, smiling,
Turned to him, told him,
"Had you said so the sooner,
You would have spared
Your spirited sorrel
A great deal of anguish,"
And she took off her veil.

Of all of the maidens
And all of the women
He ever had seen,
This was the fairest.
Powyll of Dyfed
Came to her side,

Said to her, "Lady,
Receive my greeting,
And what is your journey?"
—"I go my own errand
In my own manner."
—"Oh, what is your quest?"
—"You," she replied.

It would be a big lie
To say they were happy
For ever and ever:
Boredom, depression,
Sometimes would settle
Even in Narberth,
And now and again
The hurt of a wound
That time could not always
Stifle or soften,
But every so often
And over and over,
They would see from the mound
A wonder go by.

Appendix

(I follow the description given by Gwyn Williams, in *An Introduction to Welsh Poetry*, Faber & Faber, London, 1953. The order corresponds with that in which the poems appear in the preceding pages.)

1. Cyhydedd fer. Simply, a rhymed couplet of 8-syllable lines, well-known to us from Marvell, Herrick, and many others. The Welsh, as will appear later, are fond of using it as a base, starting with it, then breaking into combinations of 10 and 6, or 9 and 7, and so on.

2. Englyn penfyr. A stanza of three lines, of ten, seven, and seven syllables. One, two, or three syllables occur at the end of the first line after the main rhyme, and these are echoed by rhyme, alliteration, or assonance, in the first half of the second line.

3. Englyn milwr. A stanza of three lines, on one rhyme, with seven syllables to each line.

4. Englyn unodl union. A four-line stanza, ten, six, seven, and seven syllables respectively. As in Englyn penfyr, the first line has one, two, or three syllables after the main rhyme, and these are echoed in the beginning of line two.

5. Englyn unodl crwca. This is also a four-line stanza, reversing the pattern of Englyn unodl union, in that the syllable count of the lines runs seven, seven, ten, six, respectively. The same principles apply in the echoing of the syllables that follow the main rhyme in the long line.

227

6. Englyn cyrch. A four-line, seven-syllable stanza. Lines one, two, and four rhyme, and line three rhymes into the middle of line four.

7. Englyn proest dalgron. Four lines, seven syllables to the line, off-rhyming on vowels or diphthongs. The quantity of the rhymed syllables must be the same, either all long, or all short.

8. Englyn lleddfbroest. Four lines, seven syllables to the line. The rhymes must be the four diphthongs ae, oe, wy, ei. Impossible to reproduce in English, so I have had to make do with what diphthongs our language has at its disposal.

9. Englyn proest gadwynog. Also four lines, seven syllables. Lines one and three rhyme; lines two and four off-rhyme with one and three, and with each other.

10. Awdl gywydd. A quatrain of seven-syllable lines, lines two and four rhyming, lines one and three rhyming into the third, fourth, or fifth syllable of lines two and four.

11. Cywydd deuair hirion. Couplets, in seven-syllable lines, rhyming a stressed with an unstressed syllable. My "Cymric Love Song" is inaccurate, in that the lines do not contain the full quota of seven syllables.

12. Cywydd deuair fyrion. A rhymed four-syllable couplet.

13. Cywydd llosgyrnog. A six-line stanza, the syllables running eight, eight, seven; eight, eight, seven. Lines one and two rhyme with the middle of line three; lines four and five with the middle of line six; and three and six rhyme with each other.

14. Rhupunt. A line of three, four, or five sections, of four syllables each. All but the last section rhyme with each other; the last section carries the main rhyme. Each section may be written as a separate line, as in my example.

15. Byr a thoddaid. This measure combines the eight-syllable couplet with another type of couplet, called toddaid byr. The latter consists of ten syllables, then six; in the ten-syllable line the main rhyme is found before the end, as with many of the Englyn forms, and the syllables that follow the main rhyme in the long line must be linked with the early syllables, by alliteration, rhyme, or assonance, of the first part of the six-syllable line.

16. Clogyrnach. This form also begins with an eight-syllable couplet, followed by lines of five, five, three, three, syllables each, though the three, three pair may be written

as one six-syllable line. The five-syllable lines rhyme with each other, and with the first of the threes; the second three rhymes with the original couplet.

17. Cyhydedd naw ban. A nine-syllable line, rhyming in couplets, and often continuing the same rhyme through the entire stanza.

18. Cyhydedd hir. Lines of five, five, five, and four syllables (sometimes arranged as single nineteen syllable lines), the first three lines rhyming with each other, the fourth, or shorter line, or section, carrying the main rhyme.

19. Toddaid. Quatrains, alternating between ten-syllable and nine-syllable lines. A syllable toward the end of the first line rhymes into the middle of the second, and the same effect is reproduced in lines three and four. Lines two and four rhyme with each other.

20. Gwawdodyn. This form begins with the nine-syllable couplet, Cyhydedd naw ban, described above, then goes on with either Toddaid or Cyhydedd hir. In my example, the stanzas alternate in the employment of the latter two types in lines three and four of each stanza.

21. Gwawdodyn hir. This is the same as the above, except that the stanza begins with two nine-line couplets before breaking into Toddaid or Cyhydedd hir.

22. Hir a thoddaid. A ten-syllable quatrain followed by a Toddaid.

23. Cyrch a chwta. A stanza of six seven-syllable lines followed by an Awdl gywydd couplet.

24. Tawddgyrch cadwynog. The scheme is like that of a Rhupunt, except that the rhymes appear in A, B, B, C, order.

II. CYNGHANEDD. HARMONY, INTERLOCKING.

(I follow the explanation given by A. S. D. Smith [Caradar] in the Third Part of *Welsh Made Easy*, without, however, going into the complications of rising and falling rhythms, so-called.)

A. Cynghanedd Draws. In this form of cynghanedd, alliteration is required only at the beginning and end of the line, the middle portion being by-passed. "A *c*at may look at a *k*ing." Or, "he *r*ode to the city of *R*ome."

B. Cynghanedd Groes. Here, all the first half of the line must alliterate with all the second half. "*On* a *set*tee *in* a *c*ity."

229

C. Cynghanedd Sain. Two words within the line must rhyme, and the second of them alliterate, but not rhyme, with the last word. "In the *park,* in the *dark,* I *dare.*"

D. Cynghanedd Lusg. The last syllable of some word in the earlier part of the line must rhyme with the next to the last syllable of the last word, which must be a word of two or more syllables with the accent on the next to the last syllable. "Beg*in* to sing in *win*ter."

The poetry of Gerard Manley Hopkins contains many instances of the use of Cynghanedd; the poem called *Inversnaid,* in particular, might well repay the reader who is interested in studying these effects.

LATER POEMS AND TRANSLATIONS

THE THRACIAN WOMEN

"Lo, our despiser!", the Thracian women cried
Because he loved Eurydice, or men,
Or maybe only loved the art of song
Found in her presence, nourished by her loss;
And they, poor creatures, hated men, and song,
And other women. So they hated him,
And when the stones they flung fell short, in love,
They used their hands and tore him limb from limb.

Although, in rout and revel, they would toss
Their wands to Bacchus, Attis was the one
Toward whom their covert admiration went,
Whose cult they really tended. It was he
Who brought about his own dismemberment
In desperate anguish, gouging from the groin
The guilty secrets with the sharp flint stone,
And that was how they wanted men to be.

Those who hate art can never hurt it. So
The head of Orpheus floated down the stream
Still singing where the waves of Hebrus flow,
Still singing, not down any single river,
But all the shining streams of Time, forever,
Through the dark nights and during sunny days,
And rocks and trees and animals rejoice
In that pure virtue, that immortal voice.

Listen, Oh listen! We can be like these
Till even the presence of our enemies
Is matter for rejoicing, praise and praise.

FRAGMENT OF A LEGEND

And they were made aware
Of an illumination in the night,

Light where the shadows of the cypress fell,
A bright surprising presence, standing there
In flesh and robes, amid the murk of Hell.

And suddenly the lyre was raised in Hell,
As Orpheus sang. To the strange music, stronger
Than their self-torment's everlasting spell,
Came all the ghosts in myriads, no longer
Ambition-ridden, free from guilt, from dread.
Tantalus forgot his thirst and hunger;
The wheel, the rock, were still; the vultures fed
No more on Tityos. "I do not know,
I do not know," the words and music said,
"What power Love possesses here below,
But I have heard your might and majesty
Acknowledge him. Let my beloved go!
For your queen's sake, let her return with me."
The silence, as the music ended, fell
Purer than music. From Persephone,
Half smiling, Orpheus faced the lord of Hell.

Silent, the proud and luckless lord of Hell,
Dark monarch of the dark domain below,
Listened to Orpheus' song, and heard his plea,
And wept, for once not quite implacable,
Yet, being an ironic god and wise,
Knew what a lord of Hell was bound to know,
That out of loss alone the great songs rise
And knew that this musician, being free
To make the ultimate choice, would turn his eyes,
Would execute the sentence, none but he,
Loosed from the one, bound to the other spell,
So Pluto gravely called Eurydice,
Gave his false terms and watched them leaving
        Hell.

Silent, in hope and doubt, they climb from Hell,
Her trembling ghost behind him. Daylight nears.
Let them but reach the light, and all is well.

And now he knows, as surely as he fears,
Her permanence, her change, her safe remove
From the great song that drew the iron tears.
The music even the Furies paused to love
Fades into admonition—
                         Keep the ghost,
Forsake the girl.
                Song is your love.
                              If she
Is saved, you are lost, you are both forever lost.
Turn.
        Face her.
                Cry "Farewell!"
With almost all your heart, and let her be
Consigned, with everlasting love, to Hell.

FOR MARTHA FROM SALEM, 1692

Given her moment, when she might have played
The abject penitent or brazen liar
To suit the public appetite, she made
A very bad impression. Their desire
Craved visible horrors, loosed and actual,
Rank in the room, attested, verified:
"Is there a Devil in you?" "None at all
Except the one you think you see," she cried.

She faced the court, unloved, impolitic,
With no defender but a shrewish tongue,
Rude health, defiant nerve. To these the sick
Never show mercy. Wherefore, she was hung.
Wherefore, I wish her outraged spirit well,
That arrant hag, the rampant Queen of Hell.

JULY,
WITHOUT ADJECTIVES

Darken, fade,
Lichen, cloud,
Shadow on stone,
Sun over meadow.
Vireos vary
The tune, the music.

Bees hunt savor
In clover, in mint,
In thyme and currant.
The current of time
Goes by slowly.

At evening, rain
Comes down grieving
For brightness taken.
Wake at midnight,
The stars are burning.
It clears in the morning.

HEAT WAVE REMEMBERED

Breathe in this bronze; take this outrageous sun
Full on the eyeballs; never hope to look
Where willows spread, or lovely ripples run.
Even the water in the steamer's wake
Thickens like lava over ochre ground,
Thickens like mottled copper, with a shine
Too glaring, even by avarice disowned,
All red and yellow like the flag of Spain.

Along old lanes, the sheep are white and clean
The color of cloud, the cedars dark and tall.
He leadeth me, said one, by pastures green,
He leadeth me beside the waters still,
And underneath His everlasting shadow
The fiery pit will blossom as the meadow.

LIGHT RISING, WATER FALLING

The motes of brightness climb the waterfall,
The silver sparks ascending
Against the current, curve and weighted bend;
Their upward calling

Is unaccompanied, except by silence,
Except by number, toward the high
Rock of the interruption, where the moments
Pause and combine, let go

In one great pouring cataract, whose thunder
Follows its flash, whose particles of darkness
Reverse themselves in sun
To stream like fire upward against the watery arc.

"THIS GREEN AISLE—"

This green aisle
Where I walk
Alone, not always,
Only often,
Holds shade over
Cool seclusion,
Lets through sunlight
Falling on flowers.

Closer than orchard,
Soft with moss,
Here low blossoms
Cover ground,
Violets, snowdrop,
Squill, alyssum:
Most of the time
One looks down.

Still, now and again,
Overhead
Song or color
Rises higher,
Oriole, bunting,
Tanager, warbler,
Blue, red, yellow,
Orange, purple.

This green aisle
Comes to an end
In open orchard
Flooded with sun.
Here is the choice:
To go on further,
Or turn back slowly
On my old patrol.

"THAT THE SMALL RAIN—"

This fine long multitudinous unending sound
Without a hint of wind
Descends, or stands, all vertical, beyond
The open bedroom window.

And through this warp more horizontal strains
Weave, now and then, louder, and sooner die,
Cars in the street, the elevated trains,
Convairs and Viscounts toward the airport flying,

A tapestry for your chamber, softly so.
Compose yourself, my friend; be off your guard,
Completely sleep, and let the whole thing go.

The scarlet sage and cannas in the garden
Will be there in the sunshine in the morning.

THE GOLDEN COACHES

(On a *New Yorker* cover, 1954, by Charles Addams)

Where are those mountains, lying south and east,
It must be, from this flatness? In New England?
Northern New Jersey? Somewhere farther West?
Or somewhere not at all?

And what might be that thin and double line
Across their base? Would that be local fence,
Or line for power, phone, or telegraph
Running beside the highway or the railroad?

What simple questions! Think of those that rise
In the minds of this old pair, whose names are John
And Sarah, I expect, or possibly,
I'd not be too surprised, Philemon, Baucis.

Who, on their back porch, in the early light
Stand looking out across their pumpkin field
To see three golden coaches, maybe more,
Rim-deep in the black ruin of the leaves
Broken by frost from stem.

239

Three golden coaches! How could this have happened?
What good are they? What can be done with them?
The market for antiques, from Hallowe'en
Up till Thanksgiving, is a good deal slower
Than even that for pumpkins.

And that's not all. By no means. Every one
Might overnight, for all they know, from now on,
Now that it's happened once, turn into coach
Fancy and gold, instead of honest pumpkin.
They are looking none too pleased.

Maybe they will be, later. As we are,
Who, facing dark black mountain, or confronted
With fields' monotonous flatness for our outlook,
Frame-dwellers, in our plain or ugly houses,

Look out, in the chill of a late autumn morning,
With the light coming colder and slower always,
And see, for once, that something strange has hap-
    pened,
Golden and bright, and, more than that, must be there
Potential in each ordinary object.

JUNIOR

—"although a poor fielder,
he is weak at the bat."

Junior in the outfield
Wobbled at the knees,
Fighting off the fly balls
Like a lot of bees.

Bat in hand, at home plate
Junior was a fraud,
Couldn't hit the straightest pitch—
Oh my God!

Junior took the good ones,
Junior missed the signs,
Junior's feet grew tendrils,
Junior's hands grew vines.

Junior couldn't figure
That to get back home
You have to run them bases—
End of Junior poem.

BACIS

or *A Beef from Boeotia*

"The unexamined life is not
Worth living"? Ask an ocelot,
An oryx, or an oriole,
Or, even better, on the whole,
Ask one of Plato's smallest fleas.
I sometimes wonder, Socrates,
If there might not be much much too
Much of this zetetic to-do.
We ponder, probe and pry, pursue
The most elusive spoor, or clue,
Delve, winnow, fathom, sound, dissect,
Ferret, anatomize, inspect,
Glean, rummage, ransack, analyze,
Scan, view, stare (starkly), scrutinize,
Consider, question, peer and pore
Till we're too pooped for any more,
Having, by this time, figured out
Something significant, no doubt.
As for our lives, I fear, we give them
Every concern, except to live them.

I know I'm nasty, Socrates,
To file objections such as these,
But can't we strike a bargain, say,

By meeting less than quite halfway?
I, on reflection, will admit
You're not completely void of wit
(How handsome of me!); I'll allow,
Acknowledge, stipulate, and vow
The unexamined life's a curse,
A cataclysm, maybe worse,
If you, for your part, will agree
The too-examined life can be
A grim Gestalt, a wretched mess,
A narcissistic nothingness,—
Aw, Socrates, come on; say Yes!

BALLADE BY WAY OF REPLY
TO VERLAINE

"Mais moi, je vois la vie en rouge"—Verlaine
Must have been wearing spectacles of pink,
Been more than momentarily insane,
Hopped up on drugs, delirious from drink.
How could he have the witlessness to think
Men would endure this lateritious yak?
From such appalling rosiness I shrink—
I always look upon the side that's black.

I love the dark outside my window-pane.
When I see crimson, I see red, or blink.
In aspect like the Melancholy Dane
On Mother's Day I wire my mom, "You stink!"
I much prefer obsidian to zinc,
My hobbies are the thumbscrew and the rack.
And even when my wife is wearing mink,
I always look upon the side that's black.

La vie en rouge? Noir gagne. Let cloud and rain
Obscure the sunlight, let no bobolink
Sing silly tunes, but rooks and owls complain

With unmelodious omen, while the brink
Of doom extends, expands. Assassins clink
Glasses and toast destruction. At my back
I hear the deadly padding footfalls slink.
I always look upon the side that's black.

L'Envoi

Prince, don't believe a word of this. I sink
To rise, retreat in order to attack,
And even when my ledger shows red ink,
I always look upon the side that's black.

AMONG THE PAELIGNI

(Variation on a theme by Gilbert Highet)

In that calm provincial air
Noon struck out from every spire

And Sulmona's doves all flew,
Blue on white, and white on blue,

Startled, shaken, wheeling round
Down toward fountains, toward the ground

Where the poet's pedestal
Stood, not too majestical,

Still, a little more severe
Than we ought to find him here,

Hand on chin, and gazing down
At the tessellated stone,

Venus' clerk Ovyde, with these,
Venus' birds, around his knees.

PAS SEUL

On a huge black stage, and all alone, a dancer,
Under a single spot, intensely white,
Follows that fierce insistency of light
Turning as if in trance, in dream, in answer
Not to the outward music, though he moves
Apparently in time, but to a sound
Heard somewhere deep within, released and bound
By what he listens to, and what he loves.

And through this music, summer light and air
Play often, so he does not think he goes
Alone, unpartnered, through the dark, the beam
Of terrible light, but there is someone there
To share, and keep, the measure, and he knows
He moves, most sure, through neither trance nor
dream.

FOR TRIPLE ARMOR

Spell me thrice—with words, my dear,
Group eight letters, one, four, three,
In a sentence that I may
Low and musically hear.

Spell me twice—with rest, Oh deep
Under darkness, healing all
Day's untowardness in sleep.
Spell me quiet, spell me still.

Spell me one more way, my darling—
Draw the circle, near and far
All around my going, set
Runes of space for amulet.

UNDER CRAIG Y DDYNAS

"Is it day?" "No, sleep thou on."
The bell rang when the bag of gold,
Swung by accident around,
Struck it, and the warriors all
Stirred and woke, and, listening,
Heard the question and reply
"Is it day?" "No, sleep thou on."

Thousand thousands in that hall,
That great room below the ground.
They were all well-harnessed men
In their prime of hardihood.
Each in polished armor lay,
All their mail was burnished bright,
Every link and buckle shone.

Every blade was blue and keen,
Every shield gave back the light,
Thousand thousand flames of fire.
When the right arm, by mistake,
Swung the bag of gold around,
At the clamor of the bell
Every blue and ready eye

Opened wide, and every knight
Stirred himself, as if to rise;
Every arm, as if to take
Sword in hand, began to move.
One, beside whose arms there lay
Crown and sceptre, spoke his word,
"Is it day?" "No, sleep thou on."

Underneath the root of oak
Or the root of hazel, sleep
Thousand thousands in that hall
Hewn and quarried out of stone.

Armored men of hardihood
Rest in their eternal prime,
Stone and rock and flesh and blood.

Men of Arthur? Of that lord
Whose right hand was scarlet-hued?
(Owen Lawgoch was his name.)
Whose they be we do not know.
All we know is that they wait
Till the land has need of them.

Arthur's men, or Owen's men,
Under Craig y Ddinas lie.
Every blade is blue and keen,
Blue and keen is every eye.
God have mercy on their foes
When they rise and strike, but now—
"Is it day?" "No, sleep thou on."

PORTRAIT OF A POET

(After Lewis Morris, 1700-1765)

—Nawdd Duw rhag y fath ddyn!

What beggar, tinker, or sow-gelder ever
Groped more in the dirt? Look at him, with a can,
Running the streets for beer! Kind God, deliver
Us all from such a tom-turd little man!
He rolls in mire like any pig, looks wild
As any mountain-cat, without the brain
God gave an ass, or some poor sawney child
To find his way to shelter from the rain.

What poet ever flew higher? When he sings
And the right fit is on him, you can hear
Surprising composition, blending things
Richer than wine and honey, bright and clear.
What contradiction, that celestial sense
Is hoveled in this stinking residence.

PLACE NAMES

Dyfi, Teiwi, and Tywi,
Mawddach, and upper Dee,
And the black waters of Llyn Idwal
Have seen and will see
Their deal of human error,
Llewellyn's haste and grief,
The break of the mirror,
The fall of the leaf.

Crib Goch and Craig-yr-Ysba,
Lliwidd and Mynydd Maen,
Tryfarm and the Black Ladders
Over and over again
Have known of depredation,
Of rout and of raid,
And the passes, in desperation
And poverty, betrayed.

Skokholm and Skomer
Are the gray seal's breeding-ground,
Where the golden-headed gannets
Abide and abound,
Thousands and thousands, over
Those isles of the West
Whose rocks and sea-marge cover
The bones of the blest.

A SONG FOR MARDI GRAS

—Dy garu di a gerais.

I have loved loving you,
O my dear, my softly spoken.
Now the forty days draw near,
Vows are made, vows are broken.
Fare thee well, my little slim-waist—
Till Easter Monday all are chaste.

I have loved loving you,
O my fond, O my darling,
In the season and beyond,
Under moon, under star.
Now the time comes to fast—
Till Easter Monday all are chaste.

I have loved loving you,
O my linnet, O my dove.
God have mercy on a sinner!
Fare thee well and absent, love.
Moon and star go to waste—
Till Easter Monday all are chaste.

I have loved loving you,
O my green, O my shadow,
In the ambush set between
Mountainside, moor and meadow.
March, be gone; April, haste—
Till Easter Monday all are chaste.

THE DREAD

Music over. Silence. Even April
Comes this year with no more bloom than ice.
In the absence of sound
Only danger. Islands loosen evil,
Sail, oar, mast, helm, keel, prow, all black,
And the wave to the sand
As it comes once, twice,
Says nothing as it comes, then whispers *Peril*,
Whispers *Menace*. The drowned
Stir, ever so little,—
Stir, ever so little, under their green fields,
Under their ocean-floor,
Drag anchor-bones at their mooring.

Oh, they will rise, they are all of them bound to rise
Some day, and come ashore,
A great invading host, unarmed, intoning
Their thunderous inundation. To every coast
Music over silence.

THE RETURN OF PEREDWR

A battle-axe he carried in his hand,
A grown man's forearm long from helve to edge,
All silver-sharp to draw blood from the wind
And swifter than a dewdrop, loosed in June,
When dew is heaviest, from red hawthorn hedge,
And, as he rode, he heard a silver tune.

A sword, gold-hilted, with a blade of gold
He carried on his thigh; the lightning's hue
Flickered or burned all steady on his shield
Around the boss of ivory; there were
Runes on the marge, and a device of blue
Fashioned by some remote artificer.

Two brindle greyhounds ran before his ride
With sunshine on white breasts, and collars red
From shoulder-swell to ear; this side, that side,
Each went diagonal, and in their sport
Crossed underfoot as swallows overhead
Veer when a sailing-vessel comes to port.

And like sea-swallows, frightened from the shore,
The clods his courser cut rose to the sky
Above his head, behind him, or before,
Four birds, it seemed, and each one quartering
    there,
One from each hoof, to hover, bank, and fly
Forward or back, maneuvering in air.

Each corner of his purple mantle held
An apple, woven red and streaked with white,
Each of the apples, if the truth be told,
Being worth in gold a hundred oxen's weight.
Never one hair-tip stirred, so very light
He cantered, riding to the courtyard gate.

FROM LUCRETIUS: I, 1–25

Creatress, mother of the Roman line,
Dear Venus, joy of earth and joy of heaven,
All things that live below that heraldry
Of star and planet, whose processional
Moves ever slow and solemn over us,
All things conceived, all things that face the light
In their bright visit, the grain-bearing fields,
The marinered oceans, where the wind and cloud
Are quiet in your presence,—all proclaim
Your gift, without which they are nothingness.
For you that sweet artificer, the earth,
Submits her flowers, and for you the deep
Of ocean smiles, and the calm heaven shines
With shoreless light.
                              Ah, goddess, when the spring
Makes clear its daytime, and a warmer wind
Stirs from the west, a procreative air,
High in the sky the happy-hearted birds,
Responsive to your coming, call and cry,
The cattle, tame no longer, skip and bound
In joyous meadows; where your brightness leads
They follow, gladly taken, in the drive,
The urge, of love to come. So, on you move
Over the seas and mountains, over streams
Whose ways are fierce, over the greening leas,
Over the leafy tenements of birds,
So moving that in all the ardor burns
For generation and their kind's increase,
Since you alone control the way things are.

250

Since, without you, nothing has ever come
Into the holy boundaries of light,
Since, without you, no thing is ever glad
And no thing ever lovable, I need,
I need you with me, goddess, in the poem
I try to write here on *The Way Things Are.*

THREE TRANSLATIONS FROM CATULLUS

LI

What a man—no, what a godlike creature,
What a (pardon me!) super-god he must be,
Who, as he sits across the terrace from you,
Hears you and sees you

Laughing your sweet way, your sweet enchanting
Way which takes each one of my senses from me,
For, as soon as I've seen you, darling, darling,
I have no voice left,

But the tongue grows thick, and a flame is flowing
Through my limbs, gone soft, and my ears' confusion
Rings with its own sound, and a double darkness
Weights down my eyelids.

XLVI

April returns the first new-warmed chill days.
Now Heaven's wild equinox is still.
A little west wind whispers. Come, Catullus,
Forsake the prairie areas, the uplands
Too hot, too rich, too soon. Farewell, Nicea!
Time to be flying to bright coastal cities.
The mind, a little scared and much excited,
Is on its way by now. Good-bye, good-bye,
Good fellows all, whom, outward bound together,
So many different lines are bringing home.

Faring, care-worn, over so many oceans,
So many lands of strangers, as I must,
Being our father's son, I make bestowal,
Speak here, with empty purpose, to mute dust.
Taken from me by luck's peremptory malice,
Take, brother, what I bring you with my tears.
I lift my hand to you, as once in greeting,
And let it fall. Farewell, for all the years!

AFTER VIRGIL: THE TENTH ECLOGUE

Grant me this last of labors, Arethusa!
Some verses, not too many, must be spelled
For my friend Gallus; let Lycoris read them
Herself, for all I care; who could refuse
Verses to Gallus?
          Help me with the charm,
O Arethusa! Otherwise, may salt
Pollute your springs below Sicilian waters.
Sing we the loves, the troubled loves, of Gallus,
While the snub-nosed goats pull down the tender leaf-
    age.
We sing to no deaf ears, the woods reply
Answering everything.
          Now where were you,
You Naiad girls, among what upland groves,
When Gallus of unworthy love was dying?
Surely no lofty fastnesses of Muses
Caused your delay. Where were you, while the laurels
Sorrowed for him, and tamarisks wept, and pine-
    crowned
Maenalus grieved, and the cliffs of cold Lyaeus
Mourned for him lying under the lonely scar?
Look, sheep are standing all around—they welcome
Our presence. Scorn them not, O godlike poet!

Remember how the beautiful Adonis
Led sheep to pasture by the flowing rivers.
And with the sheep their shepherd came, and swine-
     herds,
A little heavy-footed, and Menalcas,
Soggy from crushing acorn-mast. "Ah, whence
This love of thine?," they are asking, and Apollo
Came with a question, too: "Are you crazy, Gallus?
Lycoris, whom you care for so, has followed,
For all I know, some shaggy soldier-fellow."
Silenus came, his rustic brow tiara-ed
With blooming fennel and big bobbing lilies,
And Pan was there, Arcadia's god. We saw him
With our own eyes, stained red with elderberries
And cinnabar. "Will it ever end?," said he.
"Such things as these Love disregards," he said,
"For Love is cruel, and no more satisfied
By tears than grasses are by meadow-rills,
Or goats by leaves, or honey-bees by clover."
But Gallus, in his sorrow, spoke: "You still
Will sing, Arcadians, to your mountains; you
Alone, Arcadians, are skilled in song,
And, ah, how peacefully my bones would rest
If by and by your music tells my passion!
Would that I had been one of you, your shepherd,
Your grape-vine pruner. Surely, if I had
A Phyllis or Amyntas for my darling,
Or anybody—(What matter if Amyntas
Is dark?—I know, *my love is dark, but comely,*
As violets are, as hyacinths are.)—She'd lie
Beside me, among willows, under the osiers,
Phyllis would gather me garlands, and Amyntas
Would sing me songs; here be cool springs, Lycoris,
Soft meadows and a grove. With you beside me
I'd be consumed by nothing else but time.
But now grim war's wild passion grips and holds me
In arms, among my enemies and their darts,
While, far from home,—ah, let me not believe it!—
Hard-hearted girl, without me you behold

The Alpine snows, the ice-floes of the Rhine.
May that cold never hurt you, that sharp ice
Not cut your delicate feet.
                              I'll go away,
And that euphoric music I composed
In happier days, I'll pipe on oat-straw now
Like a Sicilian shepherd. There's no doubt
It's better in the woods, where wild beasts house,
To endure, to suffer, and to carve my love
On the young trees, and they will grow, and my love
Will grow as they do. I'll explore the passes
With a few nymphs, or hunt wild boars, no weather
Too cold to keep my hounds and me from ranging.
Already, I imagine, I am going
Over the rocks, through sounding groves; the arrows—
What rapture!—from my Parthian bow are flying,
As if this were a medicine to heal
My rage, as if this god were ever gentle.
No Hamadryads now, no songs, can please me.
Begone again, ye woods! Our sufferings
Lack power to change him, even if we drink
Cold Hebrus water, face the snows of Thrace,
Or herd, when the bark is dying on the elm-tree,
African sheep under the August star.
Love conquers all; let us bow down before him."

These lines should be sufficient for your poet
To have sung, O Muses, while he sits there twining
A basket from the slender withes of mallow,
Gallus, for whom my love is growing hourly
As the green alder springs to life in April.

Let us arise. The shadow is a peril,
The shadow of the juniper is evil,
A threat to singers, and the shadows baleful
To the grain in the ear. You have fed enough, little
    she-goats,
The evening star is coming; get home, get home.

254

"QUID FRUSTRA QUERERIS?"

From an anonymous Latin Poet

Why, friend, persist in useless plaint
Because I was the tree I aint?
A Mackintosh, I used to be
A most remunerative tree.
Now for two autumns I have stood
Without one pome to grace my wood.
Tis not old age that wears me down,
No heavy hailstones beat my crown,
No late white frost blacked my green buds,
Not winds nor drought, fall-out nor floods,
Have drained my strength, have brought me low,
Not grasping grackle, grandma crow,
Sapsucker, starling, raven, goose,
No one of these is my excuse,
But that foul bard, who made me wear
A nest of robins in my hair.

"BE STILL, O WAVES—"

From a Welsh Poet (Anonymous)

Be still, O waves. My brother lies
Below your wildness, fathoms deep,
And in my heart the sorrows rise—
There is no stone to mark his sleep.
I hear your visitation roar,
Your onset pound, your anger cry,
As if resentful, at the shore
From which my brother went to die.

Be still, O waves. Your mournful tone
Draws from the strings of memory
An echo of a world unknown
Lamenting everlastingly.

255

A heart of rock would surely break,
My tears, more salt than ocean, spill:
One last appeal for him I make—
O listen, deadly waves; be still.

Be still, O waves. Our sorrow cries
With mortal voice across the main,
For God alone knows where he lies.
But no!—our prayer is all in vain.
Until God makes His trumpet sound
And calls my brother, as He will,
To rise with all the other drowned,
And then, O waves, you will be still.

HE GIVES UP ON THE GIRLS
OF LLANBADARN

From Dafydd ap Gwilym

I am one of passion's churls,
Plague on all these parish girls!
Though I long for them like mad,
Not one female have I had,
Not a one in all my life,
Virgin, damsel, hag, or wife.
What maliciousness, what lack,
What does make them turn their back?
Would it do them harm, or good,
Being with me in the wood?
Would it be a shame to be
In a bower of leaves with me?
No one's ever been so bitched,
So bewildered, so bewitched,
Saving Garwy's lunatics
By their foul fantastic tricks.

So I fall in love, I do,
Every day, with one or two,
Get no closer, any day,
Than an arrow's length away.
Every single Sunday I,
Llanbadarn can testify,
Go to church and take my stand
With my plumed hat in my hand,
Turn my back on holy God,
Face the girls and wink, and nod
For a long, long time, and look
Over feathers at the folk.
Suddenly, what do I hear
Rising quick and rising clear?
A girl's voice—the other one
Isn't slow at catching on.
"See that simple fellow there,
Pale, and with his sister's hair
Giving me those leering looks
Wickeder than any crook's?"
"Don't you think that he's sincere?"
Asks the other, in her ear.
"All I'll tell him is, *Get out!*,
Let the Devil take the lout!"
Pretty payment, in return
For the love with which I burn.
Burn for what? The bright girl's gift
Offers me the shortest shrift.
I must give them up, resign
These fear-troubled ways of mine;
Better be a hermit, thief,
Anything, to bring relief.
Oh strange lesson, that I must
Go companionless and lost,
Go because I looked too long,
I, who loved the power of song.

THE RAID ON CATRAETH

From Aneirin

Three hundred and sixty
Gold-collared men
Paid for their mead
In the raid on Catraeth.

The yellow mead
Was a sweet snare.
Many a year
Musicians played.

Warriors, minstrels,
Horns and goblets—
After rejoicing
Silence settles.

Their spirit it was
Cut short their days
And the power of horses,
Slim and steaming.

Gold-collared men—
Their swords were red
And their shields were white
And their spears were splintered.

Their lives paid for
Their feast of mead.
Though they were killed,
They killed also.

They slew in battle
Their number times seven.
Mothers remember
How their swords rang.

Widows were made
Before their greyness.
Short were their lives,
Long the mourning.

How many ever
Whose hands had held
The shining mead
Saw their fathers again?

Only one man,
And he no coward
Ever came home
To his belongings.

I, from my bleeding,
For my song's sake
Came back home.
I was the one.

This is my witness
Death got them all.
On Hyddwn Hill
They paid for their mead.

BRUSSELS

From Verlaine

In rose or in green,—who knows?—
Hills fade, and the slopes are gone.
All objects blend and blur
In the dusk. Street lamps are on.

Over all that is lowly
The gold of the little trees
Turns to blood color, slowly.
One quavering bird cries.

Those mournful ghosts of autumn
Are shadows, hardly more:
All the broken dreams of my torpor
Are lulled by the dull dead air.

THE ANGELS

from Rilke

They all have weary, weary mouths,
And shining souls, without a seam,
And a nostalgia, as for sinning,
Goes often through their dream.

They are almost identical,
And in God's gardens, silently
Make many and many an interval
In His might and melody.

Only when they spread their wings
They waken mighty rushing winds
As if God went, with His wide hands,
Hands like a sculptor's, through the leaves
In the dark book we call Beginning.

THE UNICORN

from Rilke

This creature never was, and could not be.
They did not know it, and, in any case,
They loved its movement, poise, and dignity.
They loved its throat, its luminous quiet gaze.
Of course it was not real. They made it so
By loving it. They left it room, always,
And in that room, that clear and open space,

It raised its head, and hardly seemed to know
The need of being. Not with any corn,
But with its own becomingness for food
They gave it sustenance and drew it nearer
Till, a pure creature with a snowy horn,
It came, all white, to where a virgin stood
And lived in her and in the silver mirror.

AUTUMN DAY

from Rilke

Lord, it is time. Summer was very full.
On the sun-dials let Thy shadows fall,
Over the levels set the winds to blowing.

Bid the last fruits be ripe on tree and vine,
Give them no more than two more days of south,
Force them to full completeness, and instil
The final sweetness in the heavy wine.

The man who has no house now builds him none;
The lonely fellow will be long alone,
And he will wake, and read, and write long letters
And wander under avenues of trees
Uneasy, to and fro, when leaves are blowing.